PostgreSQL 18 Cookbook

Third Edition

Upgrade to PostgreSQL 18 with ready troubleshooting across replication, partitioning, security, cloud provisioning, backup, and migration

Peter G

GitforGits®
ASIAN PUBLISHING HOUSE

Published by: GitforGits

www.gitforgits.com

Printed in India

First Printing: April 2026

ISBN: 978-93-49174-63-4

Cover Design by: Kitten Publishing

Disclaimer:

This book, including all its text, diagrams, and illustrations, is an original work developed for educational and informational purposes. The content is not affiliated with, endorsed by, or sponsored by or any other company, brand, or entity referenced within. All brand names, product names, and trademarks mentioned are the property of their respective owners and are used in a descriptive, educational context only. Every effort has been made to ensure that no copyrighted or trademarked material has been copied or misused in this book.

All diagrams and illustrations that are not original have been used with proper attribution and credit to their respective sources.

If you believe that any content in this book infringes upon your copyright or trademark, please contact us immediately at support@gitforgits.com. Upon notification, corrective action will be taken promptly.

Prologue

I've known a lot of database administrators, and I'm sure they've all got a memory they'd rather forget. A failed migration at the crack of dawn on a Sunday. It was a replica that just wouldn't keep up with demand, leaving customers waiting. The vacuum process was using up all the available IOPS just as the quarterly close began. We don't often talk about these things, and when we do, it's usually with a bit of light-hearted humour, like comparing scars. But these moments shape us. They teach us, more than any sunny afternoon of green dashboards ever will, what database mastery actually means. Mastery isn't about avoiding failure. It's all about being calm and collected, even when things don't go as planned.

This book is for anyone who wants to feel more confident. Not the swagger of the confident salesperson, but the kind of quiet confidence that comes from having seen a problem before, having figured out its symptoms and applying a fix you understood every step of the way. PostgreSQL 18 has some pretty amazing new features. Basically, asynchronous I/O changes how the server reads from disk. You can use virtual generated columns to model data in ways that just weren't possible before. It's been a long time coming, but we've finally got temporal constraints, OAuth authentication, logical replication slot synchronization, and time-ordered UUIDs, which are all great news for the community. To use them well, we need more than feature lists. We need the instinct to know when to reach for which tool and why.

That's exactly the kind of book I've been trying to write. So, over eleven chapters, we put together a single sample application, and we watch it grow from a simple table used by one employee into a more complex system that's divided into different parts, has backups, is secure using OAuth, and is audited. Each recipe is its own thing, but the chapters build on each other. The vacuum tuning we cover in Chapter 5 is used to inform the partitioning strategy in Chapter 6. The audit triggers of Chapter 9 feed the time-ordered event log we built in Chapter 8. The replication cluster of Chapter 7 is the same one we recover in Chapter 11. By the time you get to the last page, you'll have gone through all the stages of a real PostgreSQL deployment twice if you follow along on your own machine, and once more in the back of your mind every time something breaks at work.

From what I've seen, PostgreSQL is hands down the best database system out there right now. It's honest about its tradeoffs, generous with its diagnostics, and patient with administrators who take the time to understand it. If you don't take care of it, it'll let you know exactly where you went wrong, and often in the first line of your morning log. This book is my attempt to help you treat it well.

Give PostgreSQL the care it needs and it'll be your loyal companion for years to come.

--Peter G

Content

Preface

This thoroughly revised 3rd edition pairs every recipe with the troubleshooting know-how that separates a smooth recovery from an extended outage, walking readers through real failure modes, diagnostic techniques, and remediation patterns drawn from years of operating PostgreSQL at scale.

In this cookbook, you'll learn to set up and install PostgreSQL 18, create and design schemas, configure clusters to automatically switch over in case something goes wrong, keep your connections secure using OAuth 2.0, and perform point-in-time recovery scenarios to get your data back exactly how you left it. All the recipes work with a single growing sample database, so each one is clearly connected to the next one, just like how production systems actually develop.

This edition gives you all the tips and tricks of the latest PostgreSQL 18 features, like asynchronous I/O with io_uring, virtual generated columns, temporal constraints, time-ordered UUIDv7() identifiers, OLD and NEW values in RETURNING clauses, logical replication slot synchronization for failover, native OAuth authentication, parallel pg_upgrade with statistics preservation, eager vacuum freezing, and B-tree skip scan lookups.

You'll find concrete, tested solutions for things like troubleshooting replication lag, recovering corrupted tables, debugging autovacuum bottlenecks, or migrating away from MD5 authentication. And you'll have the operational confidence to apply them under pressure.

In this book you will learn to:

- Install, configure, and tune PostgreSQL 18 across binary and source code paths
- Diagnose startup failures, replication lag, and autovacuum bottlenecks using built-in views
- Apply new asynchronous I/O subsystem to accelerate scans and vacuum
- Design temporal constraints and virtual generated columns for modern data models
- Configure logical replication slot sync for transparent publisher failover
- Implement OAuth 2.0 authentication and migrate away from deprecated MD5 passwords
- Execute 'pg_upgrade' with statistics preservation and parallel compatibility checks
- Build partitioned, sharded schemas using declarative partitioning and Citus
- Perform point-in-time recovery and selective table or schema restoration confidently
- Audit every change with OLD/NEW RETURNING and uuidv7-keyed event logs

GitforGits

Prerequisites

This is the ultimate hands-on book for database professionals who always want to be prepared for production problems. No matter what kind of problem you're dealing with, whether it's replication lag, corrupted tables, autovacuum bottlenecks or MD5 authentication, you'll find practical, tested solutions and the confidence to implement them. All you need is some basic experience working with PostgreSQL.

Codes Usage

Are you in need of some helpful code examples to assist you in your programming and documentation? Look no further! Our book offers a wealth of supplemental material, including code examples and exercises.

Not only is this book here to aid you in getting your job done, but you have our permission to use the example code in your programs and documentation. However, please note that if you are reproducing a significant portion of the code, we do require you to contact us for permission.

But don't worry, using several chunks of code from this book in your program or answering a question by citing our book and quoting example code does not require permission. But if you do choose to give credit, an attribution typically includes the title, author, publisher, and ISBN. For example, "PostgreSQL 18 Cookbook, Third Edition by Peter G".

If you are unsure whether your intended use of the code examples falls under fair use or the permissions outlined above, please do not hesitate to reach out to us at support@gitforgits.com.

We are happy to assist and clarify any concerns.

Acknowledgement

I owe a tremendous debt of gratitude to GitforGits, for their unflagging enthusiasm and wise counsel throughout the entire process of writing this book. Their knowledge and careful editing helped make sure the piece was useful for people of all reading levels and comprehension skills. In addition, I'd like to thank everyone involved in the publishing process for their efforts in making this book a reality. Their efforts, from copyediting to advertising, made the project what it is today.

Finally, I'd like to express my gratitude to everyone who has shown me unconditional love and encouragement throughout my life. Their support was crucial to the completion of this book. I appreciate your help with this endeavour and your continued interest in my career.

CHAPTER 1

PREPARING POSTGRESQL 18

Introduction

This chapter walks us through the foundational aspects of PostgreSQL 18, laying the groundwork for effective database management, performance tuning, and operational readiness. We will start by understanding the internal architecture of PostgreSQL, gaining insight into how its client-server model operates and how its auxiliary processes maintain data integrity behind the scenes. We will then proceed through two distinct installation paths, which is prebuilt binary packages for a streamlined setup, and another is compiling directly from source code for full control over build options and custom optimizations.

Along the way, we will learn to parse and interpret startup logs, which serve as our first line of defense when diagnosing server issues. We will also explore the structural objects that make up a PostgreSQL database, including tables, indexes, sequences, views, and stored procedures, giving us the vocabulary we need to design efficient data architectures.

Finally, we will dive into the key configuration parameters that govern PostgreSQL 18 performance, including several new parameters introduced in this release such as **`io_method`**, **`io_combine_limit`**, and **`vacuum_truncate`**, alongside the significant change that data checksums are now enabled by default at cluster initialization.

Throughout this chapter and every chapter that follows, we will build a single sample application called **`cookbook_db`**. This database will serve as our running workspace, growing progressively as we add schemas, tables, indexes, replication configurations, and more in later chapters. Every recipe in this book connects back to **`cookbook_db`**, so the work we do here forms the permanent foundation for everything ahead.

Recipe #1: Simplifying PostgreSQL Architecture

Well, PostgreSQL is a sophisticated open-source object-relational database management system renowned for its robustness, extensibility, and standards compliance. An understanding of its architecture is essential for optimizing performance, diagnosing problems, and leveraging the full capabilities of the server. At its core, PostgreSQL follows a multi-process client-server model where a central server daemon called **`postmaster`** listens for incoming connections and spawns a dedicated backend process for each client session.

This architecture isolates client operations from one another. It ensures that a failure in one session does not cascade to other active sessions or compromise the integrity of the overall system.

Core Components

The server operates as a background daemon process, typically launched via **`pg_ctl`** or managed through **`systemd`** on modern Linux distributions. When a client application such as **`psql`**, pgAdmin, or a programmatic driver like **`libpq`** initiates a connection, the **`postmaster`** process authenticates the request and forks a new backend process to handle that session. Each backend process has its own memory context but shares access to a common pool of shared memory, which holds cached data pages, lock tables, and transaction state information.

This shared-nothing approach at the process level, combined with shared-everything at the memory level, gives PostgreSQL both stability and performance. The following diagram illustrates this client-server architecture and the relationship between the **postmaster**, backend processes, and shared memory.

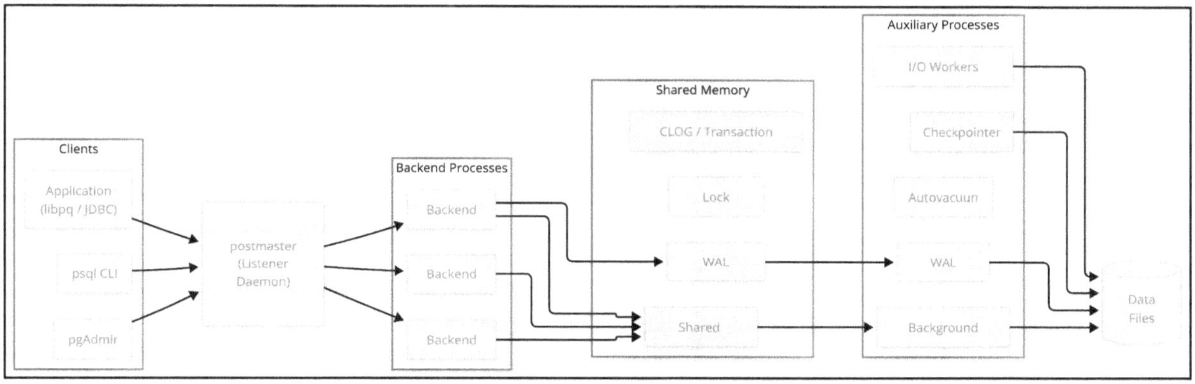

Fig 1.1: PostgreSQL 18 Client-Server Architecture

PostgreSQL relies on several background processes that run continuously alongside the main server to maintain data consistency, manage storage, and ensure durability. The **Background Writer** periodically flushes dirty pages from shared buffers to disk, reducing the amount of work the server must do during peak query processing and keeping the buffer pool available for new data. The **Checkpointer** forces all modified pages to disk at regular intervals, creating a known-good recovery point that minimizes crash recovery time.

The **Autovacuum** process automatically reclaims storage occupied by dead tuples left behind after **UPDATE** and **DELETE** operations, preventing table bloat and maintaining healthy query performance without manual intervention. The **WAL Writer** flushes Write-Ahead Log records from **wal_buffers** to persistent WAL segment files. It ensures every committed transaction is recorded before the commit is acknowledged to the client. In PostgreSQL 18, a new class of **I/O Worker** processes has been introduced as part of the asynchronous I/O subsystem, which we will cover in detail in Recipe #6 of this chapter.

Query Execution Piepline

Every SQL statement that arrives at a PostgreSQL backend passes through a well-defined pipeline of stages before results are returned to the client. The parser first validates the SQL syntax and transforms the raw query text into an internal parse tree. The analyzer then resolves object references, checks data types, and produces a query tree annotated with schema-level metadata.

The planner and optimizer evaluate multiple possible execution strategies, considering factors such as data distribution statistics, available indexes, join ordering, and cost estimates, and ultimately select the most efficient execution plan. The executor then carries out that plan, retrieving or modifying data as specified, while the transaction manager ensures that all operations respect ACID guarantees. Finally, the server formats and returns the result set to the client. The following diagram shows this pipeline visually.

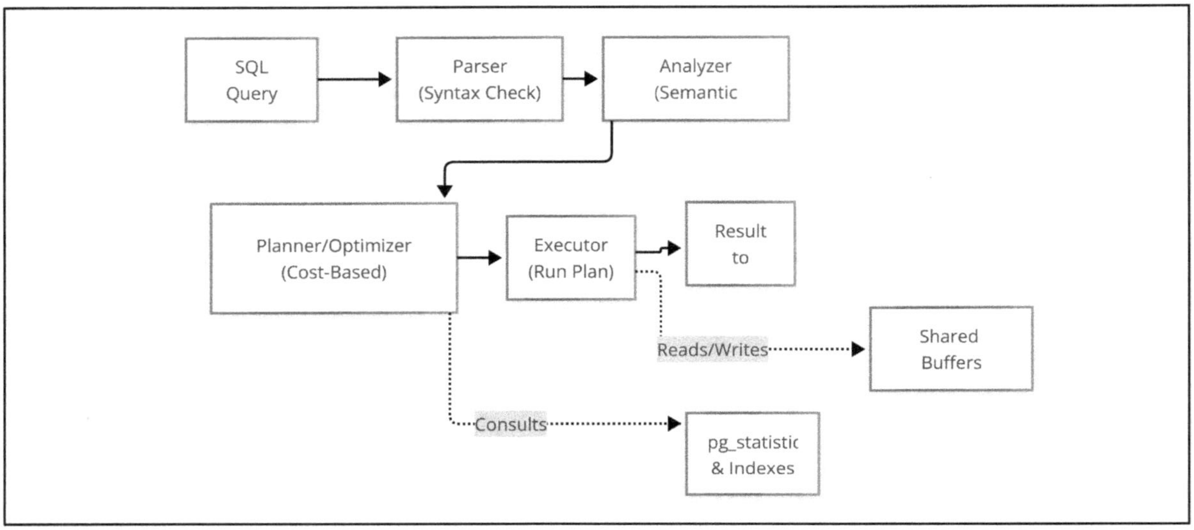

Fig 1.2: PostgreSQL Query Execution Pipeline

This pipeline helps us write better SQL queries and choose appropriate indexes, because the planner makes cost-based decisions that directly depend on the statistics and indexes we provide. We will revisit query planning and optimization extensively in later chapters when we work with partitioned tables and advanced indexing strategies.

Recipe #2: Installing PostgreSQL 18 from Binaries

The installation of PostgreSQL from prebuilt binary packages is the fastest and most straightforward method to get a production-ready server running on a Linux system. This approach is ideal when we do not need custom compile-time options and simply want a stable, well-tested installation managed by the system package manager.

Step-by-step Installation

We first ensure that our system is up to date with the latest packages and that we have the **curl** and **ca-certificates** utilities available for securely fetching the repository signing key.

For this, we will run the following command:

```
sudo apt update && sudo apt upgrade -y
```

```
sudo apt install -y curl ca-certificates
```

We will now import the PostgreSQL Global Development Group (PGDG) repository signing key and register the official APT repository:

```
sudo install -d /usr/share/postgresql-common/pgdg

sudo curl -o /usr/share/postgresql-
common/pgdg/apt.postgresql.org.asc \

  --fail https://www.postgresql.org/media/keys/ACCC4CF8.asc


. /etc/os-release

sudo sh -c "echo 'deb [signed-by=/usr/share/postgresql-
common/pgdg/apt.postgresql.org.asc] \

  https://apt.postgresql.org/pub/repos/apt $VERSION_CODENAME-pgdg
main' \

  > /etc/apt/sources.list.d/pgdg.list"
```

These commands store the GPG key in a dedicated directory and create a source list entry that references our Ubuntu release codename automatically. We now refresh the package index and install PostgreSQL 18 along with the contrib package, which bundles additional extensions and utilities:

```
sudo apt update

sudo apt install -y postgresql-18 postgresql-contrib-18
```

After the installation completes, the PostgreSQL service starts automatically. After this, we then verify the status:

```
sudo systemctl status postgresql
```

It will display following output:

```
postgresql.service - PostgreSQL RDBMS

     Loaded: loaded (/usr/lib/systemd/system/postgresql.service;
enabled)

     Active: active (exited) since ...
```

We also ensure the service is enabled to start on boot by running the following script:

```
sudo systemctl enable postgresql
```

```
sudo systemctl start postgresql
```

Post-Installation Configuration

We now switch to the **postgres** system user and launch the **psql** shell to create our sample application database. This database, **cookbook_db**, will be the single running application we build upon throughout every chapter.

For this, we will run the following:

```
sudo -i -u postgres
psql
```

Once inside the **psql** prompt, we create our database and verify the server version. In the following SQL block, we will:

```
CREATE DATABASE cookbook_db;
\c cookbook_db
SELECT version();
```

The terminal will display the PostgreSQL version string, confirming our installation is active and healthy. We will now create the first table in our sample application, an **employees** table that will grow and evolve as we progress through the book:

```
CREATE TABLE employees (
    employee_id SERIAL PRIMARY KEY,
    first_name VARCHAR(50) NOT NULL,
    last_name VARCHAR(50) NOT NULL,
    email VARCHAR(100) UNIQUE,
    department VARCHAR(50),
    hire_date DATE DEFAULT CURRENT_DATE,
    salary NUMERIC(10, 2)
    );

INSERT INTO employees (first_name, last_name, email, department,
salary)
VALUES
```

```
    ('Anika', 'Sharma', 'anika.sharma@techparts.io', 'Engineering',
95000.00),
    ('Rohan', 'Desai', 'rohan.desai@techparts.io', 'Operations',
72000.00),
    ('Priya', 'Nair', 'priya.nair@techparts.io', 'Engineering',
88000.00);

SELECT * FROM employees;
```

The query returns our three seed rows, confirming that **cookbook_db** is operational. We will continue adding tables such as **products**, **orders**, and **inventory** in later chapters as our application scope expands. At this point, we also configure remote access by editing **pg_hba.conf** and **postgresql.conf**. With this in mind, we will now open the authentication configuration file:

```
sudo nano /etc/postgresql/18/main/pg_hba.conf
```

We now proceed to add a line to permit connections from our local network using **scram-sha-256** authentication, which is the recommended method since MD5 is now deprecated. The entry looks like the following:

```
host    all    all    192.168.1.0/24    scram-sha-256
```

We then open the main configuration file to allow the server to listen on all interfaces:

```
sudo nano /etc/postgresql/18/main/postgresql.conf
```

Here, we will set **listen_addresses** and apply the change by restarting the service:

```
sudo systemctl restart postgresql
```

Verify and Rotate Logs

We now verify that the enhanced logging configuration is active by querying the running server's parameter values directly from the system catalog. We connect to cookbook_db and run the following query to inspect all relevant settings in a single pass:

```
SELECT name, setting, unit
FROM pg_settings
WHERE name IN (
  'logging_collector', 'log_directory', 'log_filename',
```

```
    'log_connections',    'log_line_prefix', 'log_lock_failures',
    'log_rotation_age',   'log_rotation_size'
)
ORDER BY name;
```

Each row in the result confirms the value loaded from postgresql.conf for our active server process. We then trigger a manual log rotation to test that the log_filename pattern generates a fresh timestamped file without requiring a server restart. We run the following function to rotate the active log immediately, which is safe to execute at any time:

```
SELECT pg_rotate_logfile();
```

The function returns true when rotation succeeds. We list the log directory afterward to confirm that a new file has appeared with an updated timestamp. This on-demand rotation is valuable during incident response, where we want to isolate the log entries for a specific time window without interrupting active client connections or disturbing ongoing transactions.

Recipe #3: Installing PostgreSQL 18 from Source Code

When we install the PostgreSQL from source code, it provides us with full control over compile-time options, enabling custom optimizations such as **io_uring** support for the new asynchronous I/O subsystem in PostgreSQL 18. This approach is beneficial when we need features that are not available in prebuilt packages or when we are running on a platform that is not directly supported by binary distributions.

Step-by-step Installation

We begin by installing the required build tools and development libraries:

```
sudo apt install -y build-essential libreadline-dev zlib1g-dev \
    flex bison libssl-dev liburing-dev pkg-config libicu-dev
```

The **liburing-dev** package is new and specific to PostgreSQL 18. It provides the **io_uring** headers required to compile PostgreSQL with kernel-level asynchronous I/O support, which we will configure in Recipe #6. We will now download and extract the PostgreSQL 18 source tarball:

```
wget https://ftp.postgresql.org/pub/source/v18.0/postgresql-
18.0.tar.gz

tar -xvzf postgresql-18.0.tar.gz
```

```
cd postgresql-18.0
```

Let us now run the configuration script to set up the build environment with SSL and **io_uring** support:

```
./configure --prefix=/usr/local/pgsql --with-openssl --with-
liburing --with-icu
```

The **--prefix** option specifies the installation directory, **--with-openssl** enables encrypted connections, **--with-liburing** activates the **io_uring** I/O method, and **--with-icu** provides ICU collation support. We now compile and install the binaries as shown below:

```
make -j$(nproc)
sudo make install
```

Post-Compilation Setup

In the following script, we will create a dedicated system user, initialize the data directory, and start the server:

```
sudo adduser --disabled-password --gecos "" postgres
sudo mkdir -p /usr/local/pgsql/data
sudo chown postgres:postgres /usr/local/pgsql/data
sudo -u postgres /usr/local/pgsql/bin/initdb -D
/usr/local/pgsql/data
```

When **initdb** completes, the terminal will display the following:

```
Data page checksums are enabled.
fixing permissions on existing directory /usr/local/pgsql/data ...
ok
creating subdirectories ... ok
selecting default "max_connections" ... 100
selecting default "shared_buffers" ... 128MB
```

An important detail to observe is the line stating that data page checksums are enabled. In PostgreSQL 18, **initdb** enables checksums by default, a change from all previous versions where checksums were opt-in. If we need to match a legacy cluster that does not use checksums (for example, during a **pg_upgrade**), we can pass the **--no-data-checksums** flag to

initdb. We will now set the environment variables, start the server, and connect. With this in mind, we will run the following:

```
echo 'export PATH=/usr/local/pgsql/bin:$PATH' >> ~/.bashrc
source ~/.bashrc
sudo -u postgres /usr/local/pgsql/bin/pg_ctl \
    -D /usr/local/pgsql/data -l /var/log/postgresql/pg18.log start
sudo -u postgres /usr/local/pgsql/bin/psql
```

Once connected, we create **cookbook_db** and seed the **employees** table exactly as described in Recipe #2. Since the installation steps for the database and table are identical, we refer back to the SQL commands in Recipe #2 for that setup.

Recipe #4: Parsing Database Startup Logs

The PostgreSQL startup logs is essential for diagnosing configuration issues, identifying permission errors, and confirming that all server subsystems initialized correctly. The logs provide timestamped records of every event that occurs during the server startup sequence, including memory allocation, checkpoint recovery, and connection readiness.

Parse PostgreSQL Logs

By default, the binary installation stores logs under **/var/log/postgresql/**, while source-based installations write to the logfile path specified during **pg_ctl** startup. We can identify the active log directory by querying the running server. We now proceed to run the following SQL inside **psql**:

```
SHOW log_directory;
SHOW log_filename;
```

At this stage, we will then open the most recent log file to observe startup entries:

```
sudo tail -50 /var/log/postgresql/postgresql-18-main.log
```

It will then display timestamped entries as below:

```
2025-10-01 08:15:32.451 IST [1234] LOG:  starting PostgreSQL 18.0
on x86_64-pc-linux-gnu
2025-10-01 08:15:32.452 IST [1234] LOG:  listening on IPv4 address
"0.0.0.0", port 5432
```

```
2025-10-01 08:15:32.780 IST [1234] LOG:  database system is ready
to accept connections
```

Each log entry contains four key components. They are **`timestamp`** indicating when the event occurred, the **`process ID`** (PID) identifying which backend or auxiliary process generated the entry, the **`log level`** such as **LOG**, **WARNING**, **ERROR**, or **FATAL** indicating severity, and the **`message body`** describing the event itself. When troubleshooting, we focus on entries at the **ERROR** and **FATAL** levels, as these indicate conditions that prevent normal operation. The following diagram shows the decision flow for triaging log entries.

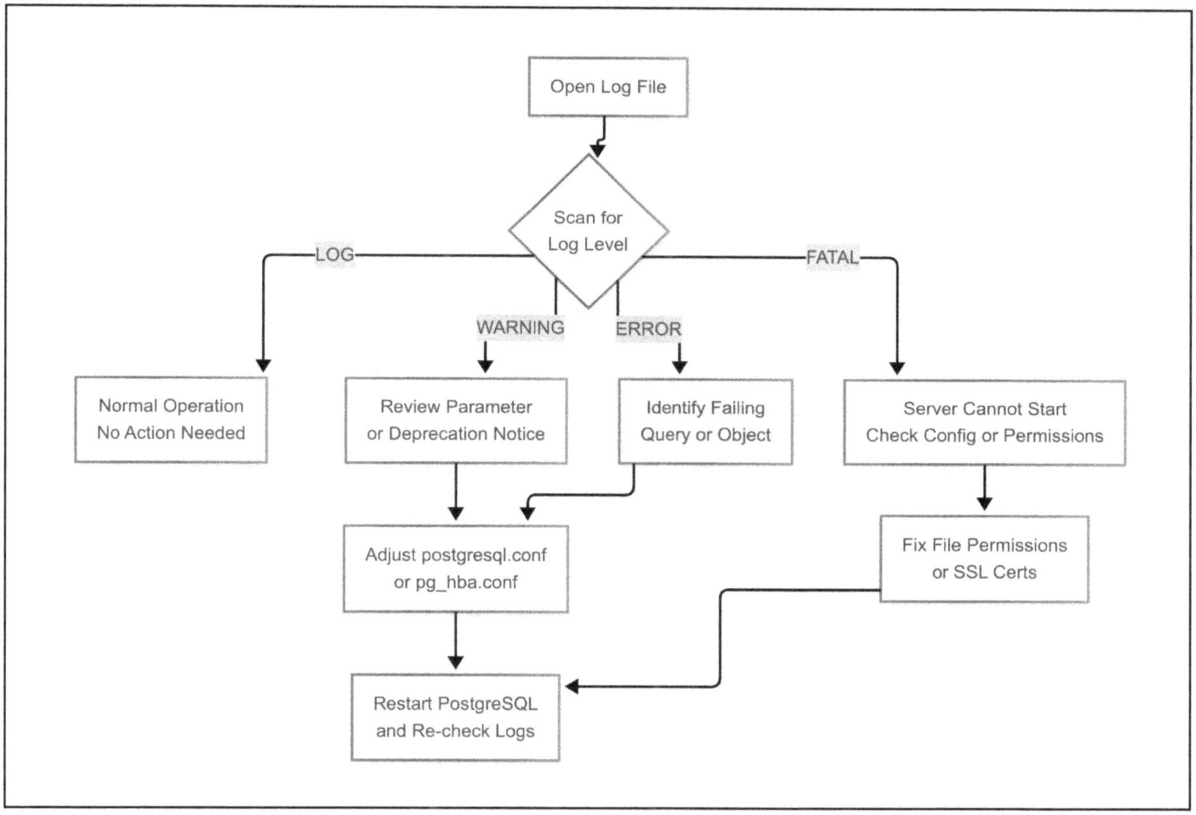

Fig 1.3: Log Entry Triage Process

Troubleshoot Startup Error

We now consider a scenario where the PostgreSQL server fails to start due to a file permission error on the SSL private key. When we open the log, we find an entry like the following:

```
2025-10-01 08:20:00.456 IST [1234] FATAL: could not access private
key file "server.key": Permission denied
```

This **FATAL** entry tells us that the **postgres** system user cannot read the SSL key file, which blocks the server from starting entirely. We fix the permissions and restart the service with the following:

```
sudo chown postgres:postgres /etc/ssl/private/server.key
sudo chmod 600 /etc/ssl/private/server.key
sudo systemctl restart postgresql
```

After restarting, we check the log again and confirm that the **database system is ready to accept connections** message appears without any **FATAL** or **ERROR** entries. This pattern of checking logs immediately after any configuration change is a habit we will maintain throughout every chapter of this book.

Recipe #5: Discovering PostgreSQL Database Structural Objects

PostgreSQL databases consist of various structural objects, each serving a specific role in data storage, retrieval, and business logic encapsulation. An understanding of these objects and their relationships is essential for effective schema design and application development. We will explore each type of object and then use **psql** meta-commands to discover them within our **cookbook_db** database.

Key Structural Objects

A **table** is the fundamental unit of data storage in PostgreSQL, organizing data into rows and columns with enforced constraints such as primary keys, foreign keys, and uniqueness rules. We already created the **employees** table in Recipe #2, and we will add more tables in subsequent chapters.

An **index** provides fast lookup capabilities for specific columns, improving query performance significantly on large tables. PostgreSQL supports multiple index types including B-tree, Hash, GiST, SP-GiST, GIN, and BRIN, each optimized for different access patterns. A **sequence** generates unique numeric values, most commonly used as auto-incrementing primary keys via the **SERIAL** or **IDENTITY** column types. A **view** is a virtual table that represents the result of a stored query, simplifying complex joins and providing a security boundary by restricting direct access to underlying tables.

A **stored procedure** encapsulates business logic inside the database, supporting procedural languages such as PL/pgSQL for transaction control and complex data manipulation.

Discover Objects

We will now connect to **cookbook_db** and use **psql** meta-commands to discover the objects we have created so far:

```
sudo -u postgres psql -d cookbook_db
```

Once connected, we list all tables, indexes, sequences, views, and functions in the current schema. We will then run the following meta-commands:

```
\dt
\di
\ds
\dv
\df
```

We can also inspect the detailed structure of our **employees** table, including columns, data types, and constraints:

```
\d employees
```

The output will then show each column with its type, nullability, and default value, along with the primary key and unique constraints we defined. As we add tables like **products**, **orders**, and **inventory** in later chapters, we will use these same meta-commands to verify our evolving schema structure inside **cookbook_db**.

Recipe #6: Exploring Key Configuration Parameters

PostgreSQL provides a rich set of configuration parameters that control memory allocation, I/O behavior, connection limits, checkpointing, and maintenance operations. Knowing how to tune these parameters is the foundation of performance optimization. In this recipe, we cover the traditional parameters that remain essential, and then introduce the new parameters that arrived with PostgreSQL 18, including the asynchronous I/O settings and the default behavior change for data checksums.

Traditional Parameters

The **shared_buffers** parameter determines how much memory PostgreSQL allocates for caching data pages in shared memory. A recommended starting value is 25 to 40 percent of total system RAM, and a typical configuration on a 16 GB server would be **shared_buffers = 4GB**. The **work_mem** parameter specifies memory available per-operation for sorting and hashing, and it should be tuned based on workload complexity, with a typical starting point of **work_mem = 16MB**.

The **maintenance_work_mem** parameter allocates memory for maintenance tasks like **VACUUM** and **CREATE INDEX**, and it is generally set higher than **work_mem** because maintenance operations benefit significantly from larger memory allocations. The **effective_cache_size** parameter estimates the total amount of memory available for disk caching by both PostgreSQL and the operating system, guiding the query planner toward index scans when large caches are available. The **max_connections** parameter limits concurrent client connections and should be balanced against available memory, because each connection consumes a dedicated backend process.

The **checkpoint_timeout** parameter controls how frequently checkpoints occur, with longer intervals reducing I/O overhead but increasing potential recovery time after a crash.

New PostgreSQL 18 Parameters

PostgreSQL 18 introduces an asynchronous I/O subsystem that changes how the server reads data from disk. The **io_method** parameter controls which I/O strategy the server uses, and it accepts three values. They are **worker** (the default), which offloads read operations to dedicated background I/O worker processes; **io_uring**, which uses the Linux kernel **io_uring** interface for zero-copy asynchronous reads (requires compilation with **--with-liburing** as we did in Recipe #3); and **sync**, which preserves the traditional synchronous behavior from PostgreSQL 17 and earlier.

The **io_combine_limit** and **io_max_combine_limit** parameters control how many pages can be combined into a single I/O request, allowing the server to read larger chunks of data in fewer disk operations. The **effective_io_concurrency** and **maintenance_io_concurrency** parameters, which existed in prior versions but had limited impact, are now significantly more meaningful under the asynchronous I/O model. Both have had their default values raised from 1 to 16 in PostgreSQL 18 to reflect the capabilities of modern storage hardware.

The **vacuum_truncate** server variable controls whether **VACUUM** truncates empty pages at the end of a table file, providing a global setting for behavior that was previously only configurable as a per-table storage parameter. The **vacuum_max_eager_freeze_failure_rate** parameter controls how aggressively normal vacuum operations attempt to freeze all-visible pages, reducing the overhead of later full-table freezing passes. The following diagram shows how these parameters relate to the I/O subsystem.

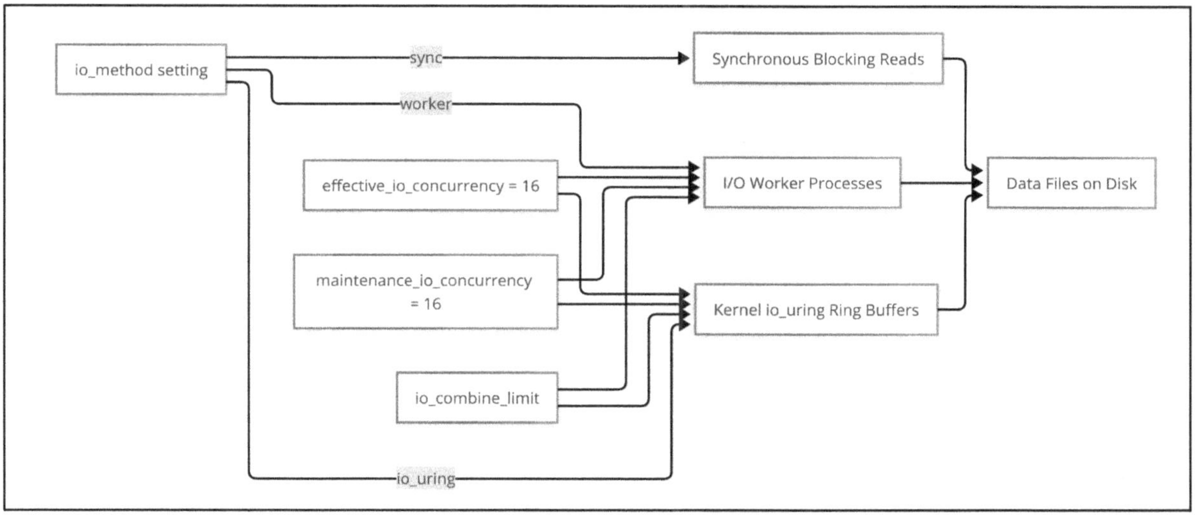

Fig 1.4: PostgreSQL 18 Asynchronous I/O Configuration Map

We can verify all current I/O settings on our running PostgreSQL server by connecting to **cookbook_db** and querying the system catalog.

```
SELECT name, setting, short_desc
FROM pg_settings
WHERE name IN (
    'io_method', 'io_workers',
    'effective_io_concurrency', 'maintenance_io_concurrency',
    'io_combine_limit', 'io_max_combine_limit',
    'vacuum_truncate', 'vacuum_max_eager_freeze_failure_rate'
)
ORDER BY name;
```

The terminal will display each parameter with its current value, confirming that **io_method** defaults to **worker** and both concurrency parameters default to **16**. If we compiled PostgreSQL with **--with-liburing** as shown in Recipe #3, we can switch to the **io_uring** method for potentially better performance on modern Linux kernels (5.1 and above) by editing **postgresql.conf** and restarting the server.

One final configuration change worth highlighting is that PostgreSQL 18 enables data page checksums by default when we run **initdb**. In all prior versions, checksums were disabled unless we explicitly passed the **--data-checksums** flag. This change improves data integrity out of the box by detecting silent corruption on disk, but the **pg_upgrade** requires that both the source and target clusters have matching checksum settings.

If we are upgrading from a PostgreSQL 16 or 17 cluster that was initialized without checksums, we must either enable checksums on the old cluster using **pg_checksums** before upgrading, or pass **--no-data-checksums** to **initdb** when creating the new PostgreSQL 18 cluster. We will revisit this topic in detail when we cover database upgrades and migrations in Chapter 4.

We will now create a concise configuration snippet that we can add to **postgresql.conf** for a typical 16 GB server. At this point, we will add the following settings:

```
# Memory
shared_buffers = 4GB
work_mem = 16MB
maintenance_work_mem = 512MB
effective_cache_size = 12GB

# Connections
max_connections = 200

# Checkpoints
checkpoint_timeout = 15min

# WAL
wal_buffers = 64MB

# Autovacuum
autovacuum = on

# I/O (PostgreSQL 18)
io_method = 'worker'
effective_io_concurrency = 16
maintenance_io_concurrency = 16
vacuum_truncate = on
```

After saving these changes, we restart the server and verify the settings by running **SHOW**

shared_buffers; and similar queries inside **psql**. The values we have configured here form the baseline for every subsequent chapter, and we will revisit specific parameters as needed when we address WAL tuning in Chapter 5 and asynchronous I/O benchmarking in Chapter 5 as well.

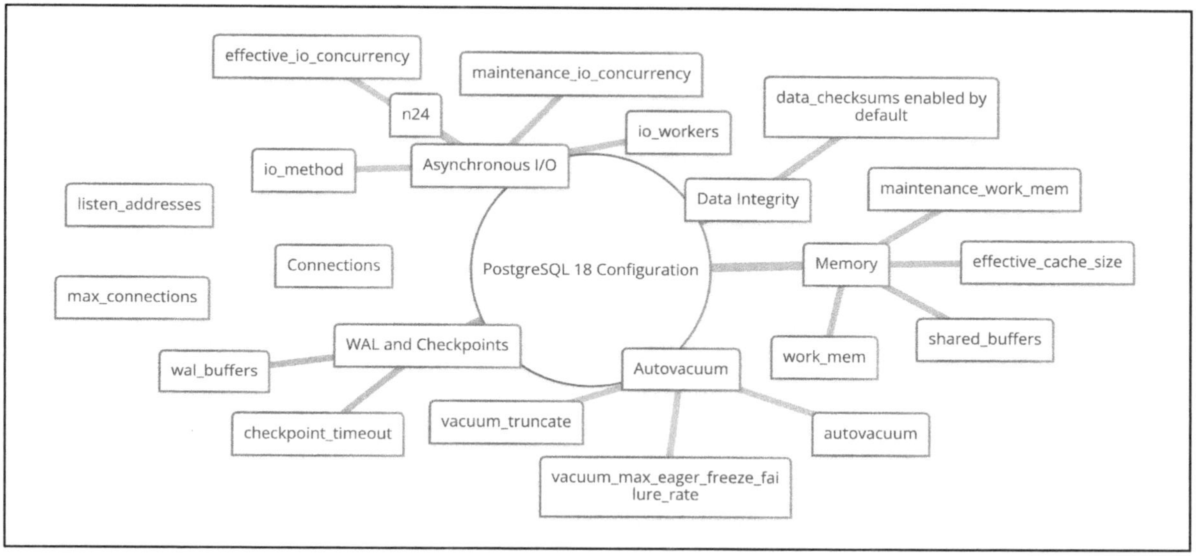

Fig 1.5: PostgreSQL 18 Configuration Parameter Categories

Summary

This chapter established the foundational knowledge and environment we need for every recipe in this book. We began by understanding PostgreSQL architecture, tracing the path from client connections through the **postmaster** daemon, backend processes, shared memory, and auxiliary processes including the new I/O Workers introduced in this release. We then completed binary installation via the PGDG APT repository for streamlined setup, and a source code compilation that enabled **io_uring** support for the asynchronous I/O subsystem. Along both paths, we created our running sample database **cookbook_db** and seeded it with an **employees** table that will grow throughout every subsequent chapter.

We also learned how to parse and triage PostgreSQL startup logs, using log levels and timestamps to quickly isolate configuration errors and permission issues. We explored the structural objects that form the backbone of any PostgreSQL database, including tables, indexes, sequences, views, and stored procedures, and we practiced discovering them with **psql** meta-commands.

Finally, we covered the key configuration parameters that govern PostgreSQL 18 performance, giving particular attention to the new asynchronous I/O parameters (**io_method**, **io_combine_limit**, **effective_io_concurrency**), the vacuum improvements (**vacuum_truncate**, **vacuum_max_eager_freeze_failure_rate**), and the significant default change that enables data page checksums at **`initdb`**.

CHAPTER 2

PERFORMING BASIC POSTGRESQL OPERATIONS

Introduction

This chapter takes us through the fundamental operations that form the backbone of everyday PostgreSQL work. We will begin by exploring the AdventureWorks sample database and using its structure as inspiration to expand our own **cookbook_db** with production, sales, and human resources schemas. From there, we will learn how to organize objects using schemas, select appropriate indexing techniques (including the new B-tree skip scan and parallel GIN index builds in PostgreSQL 18), and configure the log directory with the enhanced logging options that this release introduces.

We will also work with TOAST for oversized attributes, temporary tables, Common Table Expressions, and recursive queries for hierarchical data. Finally, we will put two key PostgreSQL 18 features into practice. One is the temporal constraints using the **WITHOUT OVERLAPS** and **PERIOD** clauses, and the other is virtual generated columns that compute values on the fly without consuming disk space. Every table, index, and query we create in this chapter builds directly on the **cookbook_db** database and the **employees** table we established in Chapter 1.

Recipe #1: Accessing Database

The AdventureWorks database is a widely used educational dataset that simulates the operations of a fictional bicycle manufacturer called Adventure Works Cycles. It provides a rich collection of tables, views, and stored procedures organized across multiple schemas that represent real-world business domains. We will install this database alongside our **cookbook_db** as a reference resource, and we will then model equivalent schemas within **cookbook_db** so that our running sample application continues to grow organically through each chapter.

Install Database from Repo

In the following script, we will download and restore the AdventureWorks dataset from the community repository. As we configured **psql** access in Chapter 1, we connect directly as the **postgres** user.

```
sudo -i -u postgres

psql -c "CREATE DATABASE adventureworks;"
```

We then download the data archive and restore it into the new database:

```
wget https://github.com/kittenpub/database-
repository/raw/main/data.zip

unzip data.zip
```

```
psql -d adventureworks -f install.sql
```

Create Schema

After the restore completes, we can explore the schema structure. The database organizes its objects into six primary schemas. They are **production** (manufacturing and product data), **sales** (orders, customers, territories), **purchasing** (vendors and procurement), **humanresources** (employee records, departments, shifts), **person** (contact details for all individuals), and **dbo** (miscellaneous cross-domain objects).

So here, we will now connect to **cookbook_db** and create matching schemas that mirror the AdventureWorks domain structure but belong to our own application. And, we will do this by running the following:

```
\c cookbook_db


CREATE SCHEMA production;
CREATE SCHEMA sales;
CREATE SCHEMA hr;
```

These three schemas, combined with the default **public** schema where our **employees** table already resides, give us a clean organizational foundation. In the recipes that follow, we will populate these schemas with tables for products, orders, categories, and departments that will persist and evolve through every subsequent chapter.

Recipe #2: Selecting Right Database Schema

PostgreSQL schemas act as logical namespaces within a single database, allowing us to group related objects together while controlling access permissions and avoiding name collisions. The when and how to use the schemas is going to be a foundational skill for designing maintainable database architectures. In this recipe, we define the schema types available in PostgreSQL and practice creating, moving, and securing objects within our **cookbook_db** schemas.

Schema Types and Creation

The **public** schema is the default namespace created in every new PostgreSQL database, and it is accessible to all users unless we explicitly restrict it. A user-defined schema, by contrast, is accessible only to its owner or to roles that have been granted explicit permissions, making it ideal for isolating sensitive or domain-specific data.

We already created the **production**, **sales**, and **hr** schemas in Recipe #1. We will now assign ownership and populate our schemas with the core tables that our sample application will use throughout the remaining chapters. At this stage, we will then run the following SQL:

```
CREATE ROLE production_user LOGIN PASSWORD 'prod_secure_pass';
CREATE ROLE sales_user LOGIN PASSWORD 'sales_secure_pass';

ALTER SCHEMA production OWNER TO production_user;
ALTER SCHEMA sales OWNER TO sales_user;

-- Move employees to the hr schema:
ALTER TABLE public.employees SET SCHEMA hr;

-- Create the products table:
CREATE TABLE production.products (
    product_id SERIAL PRIMARY KEY,
    product_name VARCHAR(100) NOT NULL,
    product_number VARCHAR(25) UNIQUE,
    category VARCHAR(50),
    list_price NUMERIC(10, 2),
    created_at TIMESTAMPTZ DEFAULT now()
    );

-- Create the orders table:
CREATE TABLE sales.orders (
    order_id SERIAL PRIMARY KEY,
    customer_name VARCHAR(100) NOT NULL,
    employee_id INT REFERENCES hr.employees(employee_id),
    order_date DATE DEFAULT CURRENT_DATE,
    total_due NUMERIC(12, 2),
    territory VARCHAR(50)
    );

-- Create the departments table:
```

```
CREATE TABLE hr.departments (
    department_id SERIAL PRIMARY KEY,
    department_name VARCHAR(50) UNIQUE NOT NULL,
    manager_id INT REFERENCES hr.employees(employee_id)
    );
```

Each of these tables references or connects to existing objects, maintaining referential integrity across schemas. The **sales.orders** table, for example, holds a foreign key to **hr.employees**, linking every order to the employee who processed it. This cross-schema relationship pattern is something we will build on when we add partitioning in Chapter 6 and replication in Chapter 7.

Verify Schema Ownership and Access

We now verify that each schema has the correct owner and that role-based access boundaries are in place. At this point, we run the following query against the system catalog to confirm ownership and access privileges for all four schemas in our database:

```
SELECT nspname AS schema_name,
       pg_get_userbyid(nspowner) AS owner,
       has_schema_privilege('production_user', nspname, 'USAGE') AS
prod_can_use,
       has_schema_privilege('sales_user', nspname, 'USAGE')
AS sales_can_use
FROM pg_namespace
WHERE nspname IN ('public', 'hr', 'production', 'sales')
ORDER BY nspname;
```

The output confirms that the production and sales schemas are owned by their respective roles and that cross-schema access is governed by explicit USAGE grants. We also grant each role SELECT on only the tables it requires, following the principle of least privilege. This ownership structure keeps data isolated by business domain and prevents accidental cross-contamination between the HR, production, and sales datasets as our sample application continues to grow throughout this book.

Recipe #3: Selecting Indexing Techniques

The process of indexing has a direct and measurable impact on query performance. PostgreSQL supports several index types, each optimized for different data patterns and query shapes. In this recipe, we cover all six index types and highlight B-tree skip scan lookups and parallel GIN index builds.

Explore GiST, SP-GiST and GIN Index

The **B-tree** index is the default type, optimized for sortable data and supporting equality and range queries efficiently. In PostgreSQL 18, B-tree indexes now support **skip scan** lookups, which allow a multi-column index to be used even when the query does not filter on the leading column. Previously, a composite index on **(category, list_price)** would only help queries that filtered on **category**.

With skip scan, the PostgreSQL can now skip through distinct values of the leading column to satisfy queries that filter only on **list_price**, making multi-column indexes useful in far more situations.

So here, we will create a composite index on our **production.products** table to take advantage of thi:

```
CREATE INDEX idx_products_cat_price
ON production.products (category, list_price);
```

The **Hash** index uses hash functions and is optimized exclusively for equality comparisons.

The **GiST** (Generalized Search Tree) index supports complex data types such as geometric shapes, full-text search vectors, and range types. The **SP-GiST** (Space-Partitioned Generalized Search Tree) index is effective for hierarchical and spatial data that can be recursively partitioned. The **GIN** (Generalized Inverted Index) is designed for multi-valued fields such as arrays, JSONB documents, and full-text search vectors.

Create GIN Index

In PostgreSQL 18, GIN indexes can now be built in parallel, significantly reducing the time required to create indexes on large tables. So here, we will then create a GIN index on a text search vector:

```
ALTER TABLE production.products ADD COLUMN description TEXT;

CREATE INDEX idx_products_desc_fts
ON production.products
USING GIN (to_tsvector('english', description));
```

On a large table, PostgreSQL 18 will automatically parallelize this GIN build if **max_parallel_maintenance_workers** is set above zero, which it is by default. The

BRIN (Block Range Index) is the most space-efficient index type, ideal for very large tables where data is physically ordered by the indexed column.

Let us now create a BRIN index on **order_date**:

```
CREATE INDEX idx_orders_date_brin
ON sales.orders USING BRIN (order_date);
```

The following diagram shows a decision tree for selecting the right index type based on the query pattern and data characteristics.

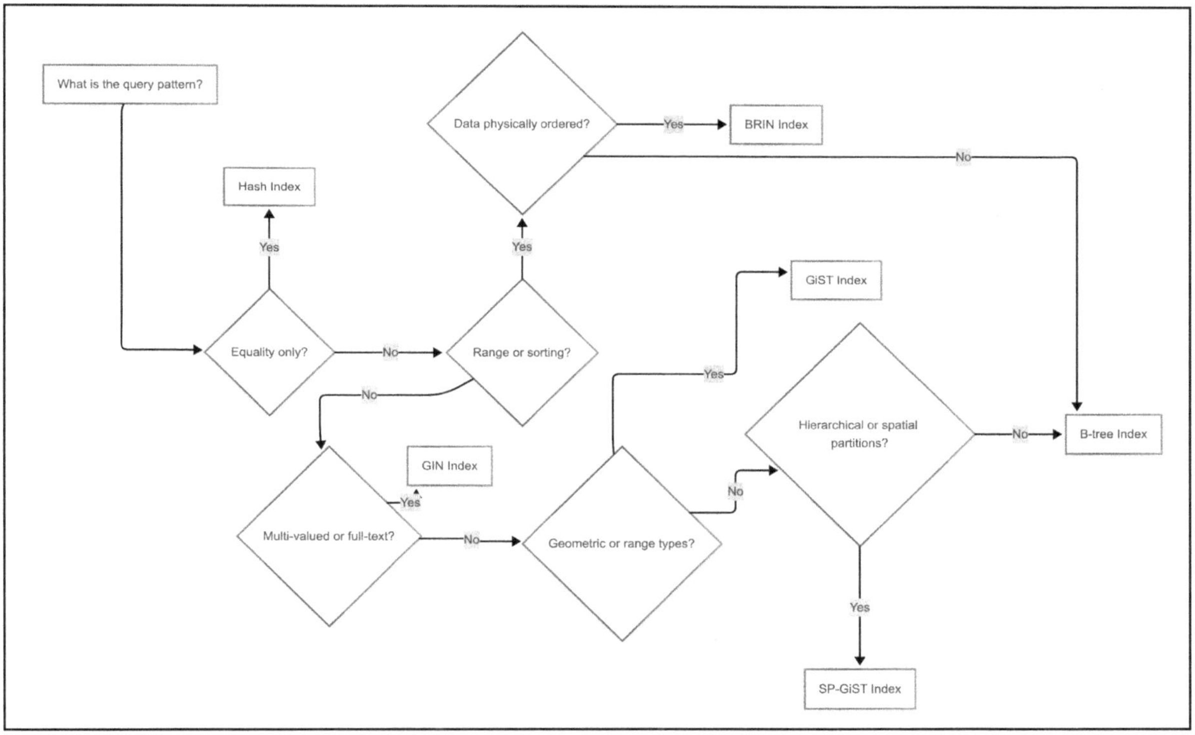

Fig 2.1: Index Type Selection Decision Tree

Recipe #4: Preparing Database Log Directory

As we configured the basic logging path in Chapter 1, we will now focus on the enhanced logging parameters that PostgreSQL 18 introduces. These new options give us finer control over connection logging, client identification, and lock failure tracking, all of which are essential for production monitoring and troubleshooting.

Configure Enhanced Logging

At this point, we will open the main configuration file for our **cookbook_db** server and add or modify the following parameters to take advantage of the PostgreSQL 18 logging enhancements. In the following command, we will:

```
sudo nano /etc/postgresql/18/main/postgresql.conf
```

So, let us add the following settings:

```
logging_collector = on
log_directory = '/var/log/postgresql'
log_filename = 'postgresql-%Y-%m-%d_%H%M%S.log'
log_rotation_age = 1d
log_rotation_size = 10MB

# PostgreSQL 18 enhanced connection logging
log_connections = 'receipt,authentication,authorization'

# PostgreSQL 18 client IP in log prefix
log_line_prefix = '%m [%p] [%L] %u@%d '

# PostgreSQL 18 lock failure logging
log_lock_failures = on
```

In previous PostgreSQL versions, the **log_connections** parameter accepted only a boolean **on** or **off** value. PostgreSQL 18 expands this to accept a comma-separated list of connection stages, allowing us to selectively log **receipt** (when the connection arrives), **authentication** (when credentials are verified), and **authorization** (when the role is resolved). This granularity reduces log noise in high-throughput environments while still capturing the stages we care about most.

The **%L** escape in **log_line_prefix** is another PostgreSQL 18 addition that outputs the client IP address directly, giving us immediate visibility into which host generated a particular log entry without parsing additional fields. The **log_lock_failures** parameter, when enabled, records every lock acquisition failure triggered by **SELECT ... NOWAIT** and similar non-blocking lock requests, helping us identify concurrency bottlenecks in our application.

With this in mind, we will now apply the changes by restarting the service:

```
sudo systemctl restart postgresql
```

Verify and Rotate Logs

We now verify that the enhanced logging configuration is active by querying the running server's parameter values directly from the system catalog. We connect to cookbook_db and run the following query to inspect all relevant settings in a single pass:

```
SELECT name, setting, unit
FROM pg_settings
WHERE name IN (
  'logging_collector', 'log_directory', 'log_filename',
  'log_connections',   'log_line_prefix', 'log_lock_failures',
  'log_rotation_age',  'log_rotation_size'
)
ORDER BY name;
```

Each row in the result confirms the value loaded from postgresql.conf for our active server process. We then trigger a manual log rotation to test that the log_filename pattern generates a fresh timestamped file without requiring a server restart. We run the following function to rotate the active log immediately, which is safe to execute at any time during operation:

```
SELECT pg_rotate_logfile();
```

The function returns true when rotation succeeds. We then list the log directory afterward to confirm that a new file has appeared with an updated timestamp. At this stage, we also verify that the log_lock_failures parameter is recording lock contention events by simulating a brief lock conflict in a test session and then inspecting the log output. This on-demand rotation is valuable during incident response, where we want to isolate log entries for a specific time window without interrupting active client connections or disturbing ongoing transactions in our cookbook_db environment.

Recipe #5: Using PostgreSQL TOAST

PostgreSQL TOAST (The Oversized-Attribute Storage Technique) is a built-in mechanism that handles storage of large field values by automatically compressing and slicing them into smaller chunks stored in a companion TOAST table. This process is transparent to the user and activates whenever a row exceeds the page size threshold, which is typically around 2 KB for a given column value. We will demonstrate TOAST behavior by inserting large text values into our

production.products table.

Working with TOAST

At this stage, we will then insert several rows with substantial description values into our products table to trigger TOAST storage.

```
INSERT INTO production.products (product_name, product_number, category, list_price, description)
VALUES
('Mountain Bike Pro', 'MB-PRO-100', 'Bikes', 2499.99, repeat('High-performance mountain bike with advanced suspension. ', 200)),
('Road Racer Elite', 'RR-ELT-200', 'Bikes', 3199.99, repeat('Lightweight carbon frame designed for competitive road cycling. ', 200)),
('Touring Helmet', 'TH-STD-300', 'Accessories', 89.99, repeat('Certified safety helmet with adjustable ventilation system. ', 200));
```

Each **repeat()** call generates a string exceeding 8 KB, which forces PostgreSQL to TOAST the **description** column automatically. We can verify that TOAST tables exist for our relation by querying the system catalog as shown below:

```
SELECT c.relname AS main_table, t.relname AS toast_table
FROM pg_class c
JOIN pg_class t ON t.oid = c.reltoastrelid
WHERE c.relname = 'products';
```

The result confirms that PostgreSQL created a companion TOAST table. This automatic management of oversized attributes means we do not need to build custom chunking logic at the application level, and we can store arbitrarily large **TEXT**, **BYTEA**, or **JSONB** values without modifying our schema design.

Inspect TOAST Configuration

We now examine how PostgreSQL has configured TOAST storage for the products table by querying the system catalog to inspect the storage strategy assigned to each column. At this stage, we run the following query to see the strategy for every column in the table:

```
SELECT attname AS column_name,
       CASE attstorage
```

```
        WHEN 'p' THEN 'PLAIN'
        WHEN 'e' THEN 'EXTERNAL'
        WHEN 'm' THEN 'MAIN'
        WHEN 'x' THEN 'EXTENDED'
    END AS toast_strategy
FROM pg_attribute
JOIN pg_class ON pg_class.oid = pg_attribute.attrelid
WHERE pg_class.relname = 'products'
  AND attnum > 0
  AND NOT attisdropped
ORDER BY attnum;
```

The EXTENDED strategy on the description column confirms that PostgreSQL will both compress and externalize that value whenever it exceeds the storage threshold. The PLAIN strategy on columns such as product_id and list_price means those values are stored inline and never compressed or moved to the TOAST table.

These tuning of TOAST strategies matters for tables that store large text, JSONB documents, or binary data, because the wrong strategy can lead to excessive bloat in the main table heap or prevent effective compression of frequently queried large columns as our products catalog grows throughout the book.

Recipe #6: Creating and Administering Temporary Tables

Temporary tables store transient data that persists only for the duration of a database session or transaction. They are valuable for staging intermediate results during complex analytical queries without affecting permanent tables. In this recipe, we create temporary tables within **cookbook_db** and highlight an important behavioral change introduced in PostgreSQL 18.

Create and use Temporary Tables

So here, we will then create a temporary table that captures a filtered snapshot of our sales data for analysis:

```
CREATE TEMP TABLE temp_high_value_orders AS
SELECT order_id, customer_name, total_due, order_date
FROM sales.orders
WHERE total_due > 1000;
```

```
SELECT * FROM temp_high_value_orders ORDER BY total_due DESC;
DROP TABLE IF EXISTS temp_high_value_orders;
```

Unlogged Partitioned Tables Disallowed

One important behavioral change in PostgreSQL 18 that affects temporary and transient data strategies is the removal of support for unlogged partitioned tables. In previous versions, the **ALTER TABLE SET UNLOGGED** command on a partitioned table silently did nothing, and creating an unlogged partitioned table did not propagate the unlogged status to its child partitions, leading to inconsistent behavior. PostgreSQL 18 now explicitly disallows unlogged partitioned tables, so that the **UNLOGGED** property is always consistent across the partition hierarchy.

If we need transient partitioned data that does not require WAL protection, we should use temporary tables or redesign the partitioning strategy to use non-partitioned unlogged tables instead.

Recipe #7: Using SELECT in WITH Queries

The **WITH** clause, also known as a Common Table Expression (CTE), defines a named temporary result set that can be referenced within the main query. CTEs break complex logic into readable, modular steps and can be reused multiple times within the same statement. We will use CTEs to analyze sales data in our **cookbook_db**.

Build CTEs for Sales Analysis

We first seed our sales table with sample data so that our queries return meaningful results:

```
INSERT INTO sales.orders (customer_name, employee_id, order_date, total_due, territory)
VALUES
('TechCorp India', 1, '2025-06-15', 15200.00, 'South Asia'),
('VeloCity GmbH', 2, '2025-06-15', 8400.00, 'Europe'),
('PedalForce LLC', 1, '2025-07-01', 22000.00, 'North America'),
('CycleHub AU', 3, '2025-07-10', 11500.00, 'Asia Pacific'),
('BikeWorld UK', 2, '2025-07-10', 9700.00, 'Europe');
```

We will now write a multi-CTE query that calculates territory-level sales totals and then ranks them:

```
WITH territory_sales AS (
    SELECT territory, SUM(total_due) AS total_revenue, COUNT(*) AS
order_count
    FROM sales.orders
    GROUP BY territory
),
ranked_territories AS (
    SELECT territory, total_revenue, order_count,
           RANK() OVER (ORDER BY total_revenue DESC) AS
revenue_rank
    FROM territory_sales
)
SELECT territory, total_revenue, order_count, revenue_rank
FROM ranked_territories
ORDER BY revenue_rank;
```

The first CTE **territory_sales** aggregates revenue and order counts by territory. The second CTE **ranked_territories** applies a window function to assign a rank based on descending revenue. The final **SELECT** presents the ranked results. This modular approach makes the logic easy to follow and simple to modify if we need to add additional filters or calculations later. We will use this same CTE pattern extensively in later chapters when analyzing partitioned data in Chapter 6 and monitoring replication lag in Chapter 7.

Materialize CTEs for Performance

We now explore how PostgreSQL handles CTE evaluation and when we should force materialization to improve plan predictability. By default, PostgreSQL may inline a non-recursive CTE as a subquery if the planner determines it is cheaper to do so. We can override this behavior using the MATERIALIZED keyword to ensure the CTE is evaluated exactly once and its result is stored before the outer query runs. We now write a materialized version of our territory analysis:

```
WITH MATERIALIZED territory_sales AS (
    SELECT territory,
           SUM(total_due) AS total_revenue,
           COUNT(*)       AS order_count
    FROM sales.orders
```

```
    GROUP BY territory
)
SELECT territory, total_revenue, order_count
FROM territory_sales
WHERE total_revenue > 10000
ORDER BY total_revenue DESC;
```

The MATERIALIZED keyword prevents the planner from inlining the CTE even when it is referenced only once. This approach is especially valuable when the CTE contains non-deterministic functions, when it is referenced multiple times in the outer query, or when we want to isolate the aggregation step from the optimizer's join reordering decisions. For our cookbook_db queries, materialized CTEs give us a stable and predictable execution plan as the sales.orders table grows in volume across the chapters that follow.

Recipe #8: Running Recursive Queries

PostgreSQL supports recursive queries too, through the **WITH RECURSIVE** clause, which allows a query to reference its own output iteratively. This technique is essential for traversing hierarchical data structures such as organizational charts, category trees, and bill-of-materials relationships.

Build Department Hierarchy

We first add a **parent_department_id** column and additional rows to our **hr.departments** table to create a hierarchy:

```
ALTER TABLE hr.departments ADD COLUMN parent_department_id INT
    REFERENCES hr.departments(department_id);

INSERT INTO hr.departments (department_name, parent_department_id)
VALUES
('Engineering', NULL),
('Backend Team', (SELECT department_id FROM hr.departments WHERE
department_name = 'Engineering')),
('Frontend Team', (SELECT department_id FROM hr.departments WHERE
department_name = 'Engineering')),
('Operations', NULL),
```

```
('DevOps', (SELECT department_id FROM hr.departments WHERE
department_name = 'Operations'));
```

We will now write a recursive query that traverses this hierarchy from the top-level departments down to every sub-department, tracking the depth at each level. In the following SQL block:

```
WITH RECURSIVE dept_tree AS (
    SELECT department_id, department_name, parent_department_id, 1
AS depth
    FROM hr.departments
    WHERE parent_department_id IS NULL

    UNION ALL

    SELECT d.department_id, d.department_name,
d.parent_department_id, dt.depth + 1
    FROM hr.departments d
    JOIN dept_tree dt ON dt.department_id = d.parent_department_id
)
SELECT department_name, depth
FROM dept_tree
ORDER BY depth, department_name;
```

The base case selects all top-level departments where **parent_department_id** is **NULL**. The recursive term then joins back to the **hr.departments** table using the previously found **department_id** values as parent references, incrementing the depth counter at each level. The recursion continues until no more child departments are found. The following diagram visualizes how the recursive query traverses this tree structure.

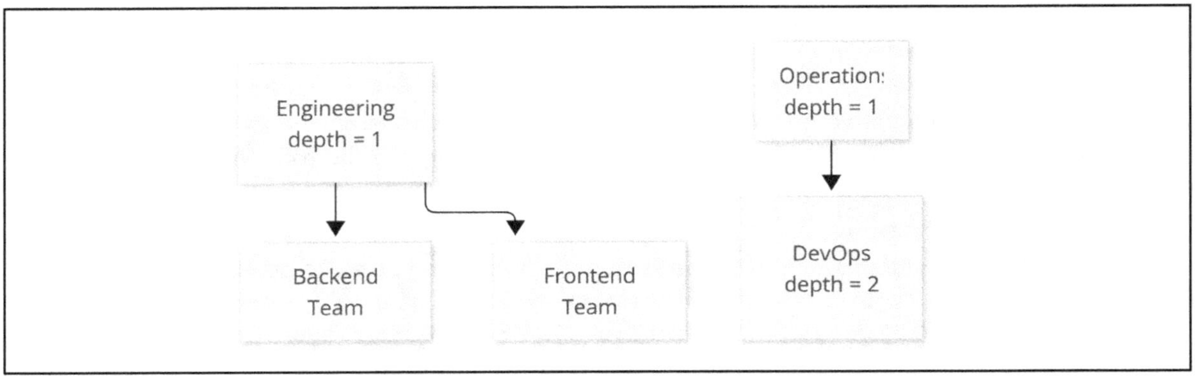

Fig 2.2: Recursive Department Hierarchy Traversal

This pattern is directly applicable to any tree-structured data in our application, and we will reuse it when we work with product category hierarchies in later chapters.

Prevent Cycles in Recursive Queries

We now add cycle detection to our recursive query using the CYCLE clause, which PostgreSQL supports as part of the SQL standard. Without cycle detection, a malformed hierarchy containing a circular reference such as a department that is its own ancestor would cause the recursive query to loop indefinitely. We rewrite the department traversal with explicit cycle protection by adding the CYCLE clause to the WITH RECURSIVE block:

```
WITH RECURSIVE dept_tree AS (
    SELECT department_id, department_name,
           parent_department_id, 1 AS depth
    FROM hr.departments
    WHERE parent_department_id IS NULL
    UNION ALL
    SELECT d.department_id, d.department_name,
           d.parent_department_id, dt.depth + 1
    FROM hr.departments d
    JOIN dept_tree dt ON dt.department_id = d.parent_department_id
)
CYCLE department_id SET is_cycle USING path
SELECT department_name, depth, is_cycle
FROM dept_tree
```

```
ORDER BY depth, department_name;
```

The CYCLE clause monitors the department_id column across recursive iterations and sets the is_cycle boolean to true whenever the same value reappears in the traversal path. The USING path clause maintains an array of visited node identifiers so that each iteration can detect repetition without a full table scan. Any row where is_cycle evaluates to true indicates a circular reference in our data, which we can then investigate and correct before it reaches a production deployment. This cycle-detection pattern applies wherever we traverse tree-structured data in our application.

Recipe #9: Working with Temporal Constraints

PostgreSQL 18 introduces temporal constraints, a powerful new capability that allows us to enforce data integrity rules over time periods directly in our schema definition. Before this release, preventing overlapping time ranges for the same entity required application-level logic or hand-crafted exclusion constraints. The new **WITHOUT OVERLAPS** clause for **PRIMARY KEY** and **UNIQUE** constraints, along with the **PERIOD** clause for **FOREIGN KEY** constraints, brings this functionality into the database engine itself using native range types.

Enforce Non-Overlapping Periods

We will model employee project assignments in our **cookbook_db** where each employee can be assigned to only one project at any given time. We first enable the **btree_gist** extension, which temporal constraints require for their underlying GiST index support.

```
CREATE EXTENSION IF NOT EXISTS btree_gist;
```

We will now create a **project_assignments** table that uses a **daterange** column and a **PRIMARY KEY** with the **WITHOUT OVERLAPS** clause to prevent any employee from having overlapping assignments.

With this in mind, we will now run the following query:

```
CREATE TABLE hr.project_assignments (
    employee_id INT NOT NULL REFERENCES hr.employees(employee_id),
    project_name VARCHAR(100) NOT NULL,
    assignment_period daterange NOT NULL,
    PRIMARY KEY (employee_id, assignment_period WITHOUT OVERLAPS)
    );
```

The **WITHOUT OVERLAPS** keyword tells PostgreSQL that for any given **employee_id**, the **assignment_period** ranges must never overlap. Behind the scenes, this behaves like an exclusion constraint using a GiST index, but the syntax is far cleaner and more declarative. We will now insert valid non-overlapping assignments:

```
INSERT INTO hr.project_assignments (employee_id, project_name,
assignment_period)
VALUES
(1, 'Database Migration', daterange('2025-01-01', '2025-06-30')),
(1, 'Cloud Infrastructure', daterange('2025-07-01', '2025-12-31')),
(2, 'API Gateway', daterange('2025-03-01', '2025-09-30'));
```

If we now attempt to insert an assignment for employee 1 that overlaps with an existing period, PostgreSQL will reject it immediately. At this stage, we will then run the following SQL to test the constraint:

```
INSERT INTO hr.project_assignments (employee_id, project_name,
assignment_period)
VALUES (1, 'Security Audit', daterange('2025-05-01', '2025-08-
31'));
```

The terminal shall throw the following error:

```
ERROR:  conflicting key value violates exclusion constraint
        "project_assignments_pkey"
DETAIL:  Key (employee_id, assignment_period)=(1, [2025-05-01,2025-
08-31))
         conflicts with existing key (employee_id,
assignment_period)=
         (1, [2025-01-01,2025-06-30)).
```

Temporal Foreign Keys with PERIOD

PostgreSQL 18 also introduces temporal foreign keys using the **PERIOD** clause, which ensures referential integrity across time ranges by checking for range containment rather than simple equality.

Here, we will create a **project_milestones** table that references **project_assignments** as shown below:

```
CREATE TABLE hr.project_milestones (
    milestone_id SERIAL PRIMARY KEY,
```

```
    employee_id INT NOT NULL,
    milestone_date daterange NOT NULL,
    milestone_name VARCHAR(100) NOT NULL,
    FOREIGN KEY (employee_id, PERIOD milestone_date)
        REFERENCES hr.project_assignments (employee_id, PERIOD
assignment_period)
    );
```

The **PERIOD** keyword instructs PostgreSQL to verify that the **milestone_date** range is fully contained within a valid **assignment_period** for the same **employee_id**. If we attempt to insert a milestone that falls outside any assignment period, the database will reject it, guaranteeing temporal referential integrity without any application-level validation. The following diagram illustrates how **WITHOUT OVERLAPS** and **PERIOD** work together across two related tables.

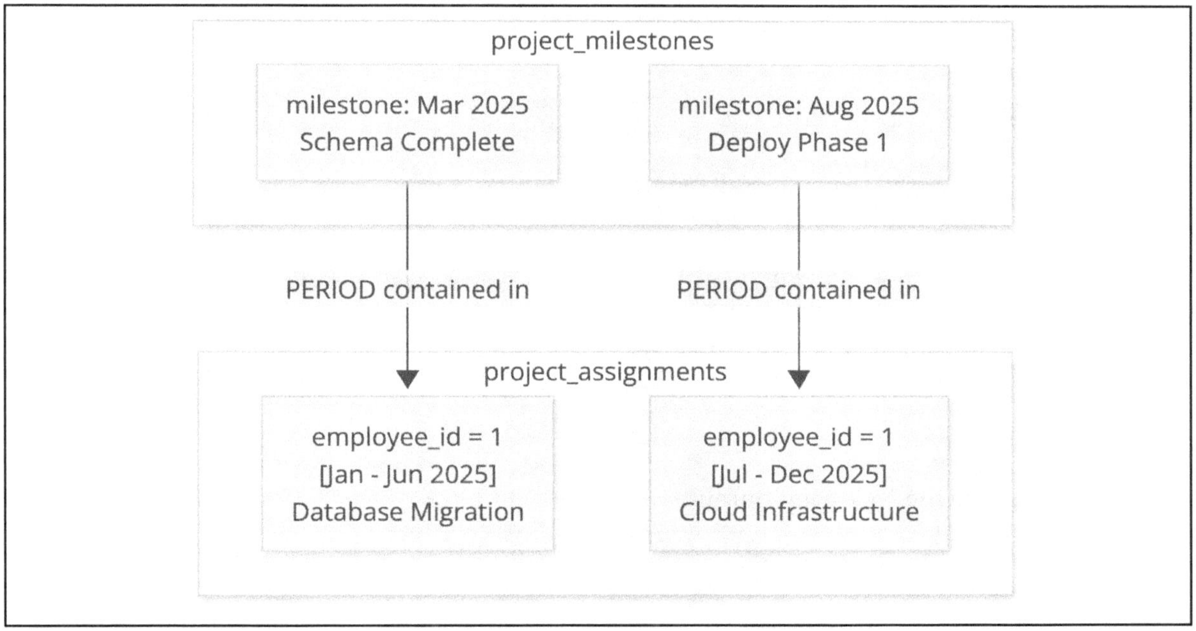

Fig 2.3: Temporal Foreign Key with PERIOD Clause

Recipe #10: Using Virtual Generated Columns

PostgreSQL 18 introduces virtual generated columns, a new kind of computed column that calculates its value at query time rather than storing a precomputed result on disk. In previous versions, all generated columns were of the **STORED** type, meaning the computed value was written to disk during **INSERT** or **UPDATE** operations and occupied storage like any regular column. The virtual generated columns reverse this trade-off. They consume zero disk space and are always up to date, because the expression is evaluated every time the column is read.

With PostgreSQL 18, the **VIRTUAL** type is the default when we omit the **STORED** or **VIRTUAL** keyword. It therefore aligns PostgreSQL with the behavior of several other database systems.

Create Virtual Generated Columns

We will add two virtual generated columns to our **hr.employees** table, one that concatenates the first and last name into a full name, and another that computes an annual bonus at 10 percent of the salary.

Following SQL is what we will run:

```
ALTER TABLE hr.employees
ADD COLUMN full_name VARCHAR
    GENERATED ALWAYS AS (first_name || ' ' || last_name);

ALTER TABLE hr.employees
ADD COLUMN annual_bonus NUMERIC(10, 2)
    GENERATED ALWAYS AS (salary * 0.10);
```

Because we omitted the **STORED** and **VIRTUAL** keywords, the PostgreSQL defaults to **VIRTUAL** for both columns. We will then verify the result by querying the table as below:

```
SELECT employee_id, full_name, salary, annual_bonus
FROM hr.employees;
```

It will then produce the following output:

```
employee_id |     full_name     |  salary   | annual_bonus
-------------+------------------+----------+--------------
           1 | Anika Sharma     | 95000.00 |       9500.00
           2 | Rohan Desai      | 72000.00 |       7200.00
           3 | Priya Nair       | 88000.00 |       8800.00
```

Both **full_name** and **annual_bonus** are computed on the fly from the underlying **first_name**, **last_name**, and **salary** columns. If we update a salary, the bonus recalculates automatically without any trigger or additional write. We verify this by updating one row. We run the following

```
SQL:UPDATE hr.employees SET salary = 98000.00 WHERE employee_id = 1;

SELECT full_name, salary, annual_bonus FROM hr.employees WHERE employee_id = 1;
```

The annual_bonus now shows 9800.00, reflecting the updated salary instantly.

Select Virtual vs. Stored

Virtual columns are ideal when the expression is lightweight, the column is not frequently filtered or sorted in large-scale queries, and we want to minimize disk footprint. Stored generated columns remain the better choice when we need to create an index on the computed value, because virtual columns cannot be indexed in PostgreSQL 18. Stored columns are also required for logical replication scenarios, as virtual columns are not replicated. The following diagram summarizes the decision points between the two types

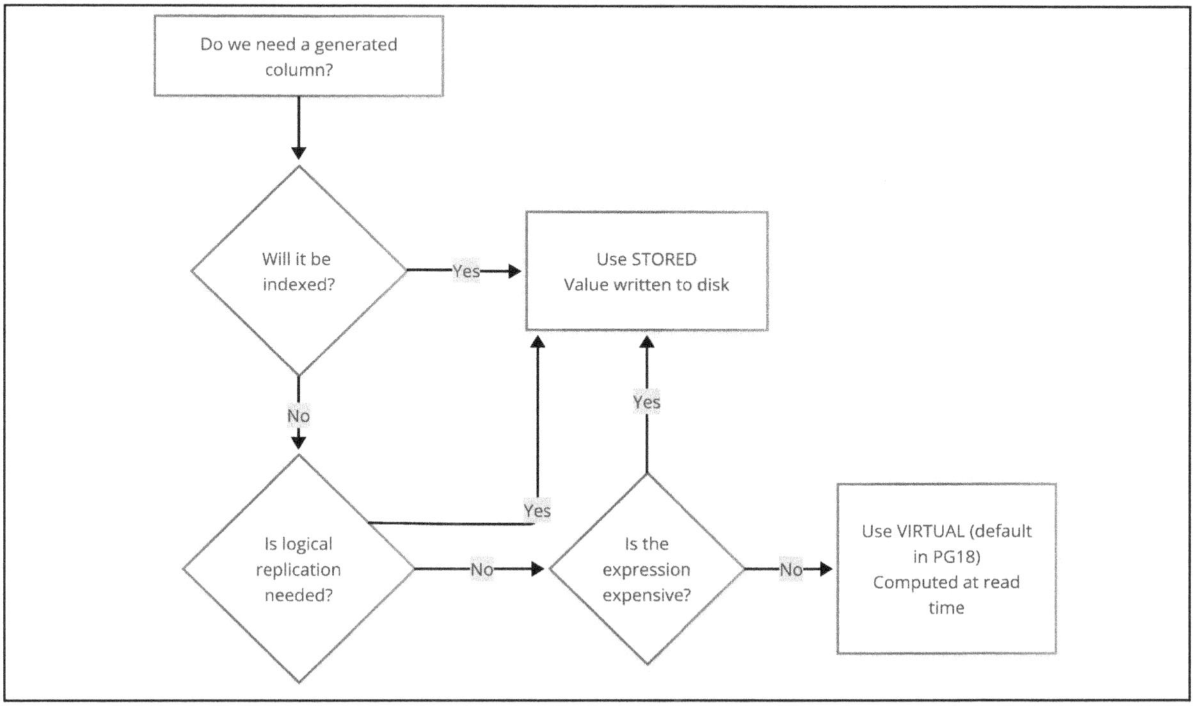

Fig 2.4: Virtual vs Stored Generated Column Decision

We will revisit the distinction between virtual and stored columns when we configure logical replication in Chapter 7 and when we add performance-critical indexes in later chapters.

Summary

This chapter expanded our **cookbook_db** from a single **employees** table into a multi-schema application with **production**, **sales**, and **hr** namespaces, along with tables for products, orders, departments, project assignments, and milestones. We explored the AdventureWorks database as a reference model and then built equivalent structures within our own application to maintain sample continuity across the entire book.

We practiced selecting the right index type for each query pattern and learned how PostgreSQL 18 extends indexing with B-tree skip scan lookups and parallel GIN index builds. We configured the log directory using the new granular **log_connections** options, the **%L** client IP escape in **log_line_prefix**, and the **log_lock_failures** parameter, all of which are new in this release. We worked with TOAST storage, temporary tables, CTEs, and recursive queries for hierarchical traversal, establishing patterns we will reuse throughout subsequent chapters.

Most significantly, we put two headline PostgreSQL 18 features into practice. We used temporal constraints with **WITHOUT OVERLAPS** and **PERIOD** to enforce non-overlapping project assignments and temporal referential integrity at the schema level. We also created virtual generated columns that compute values at read time without consuming disk space, replacing the stored-only model from previous versions.

CHAPTER 3
POSTGRESQL CLOUD PROVISIONING

Introduction

This chapter walks us through provisioning and managing PostgreSQL in the cloud using Amazon Web Services (AWS). We will create a PostgreSQL instance on Amazon RDS, connect to it through an EC2 instance, and perform backup and restore operations using native PostgreSQL tools and Amazon S3. We will also configure connection pooling with **pgbouncer**, implement read replication for horizontal scalability, and configure bi-directional replication using the **pglogical** extension.

Every recipe in this chapter connects to the **cookbook_db** sample application we built in Chapters 1 and 2, extending it into a cloud-hosted environment that reflects real production workloads. All AWS CLI commands, connection strings, and configuration files target an Ubuntu 24.04 LTS EC2 instance running alongside our RDS deployment. We assume an active AWS account and sufficient IAM permissions to create RDS instances, EC2 instances, S3 buckets, and security groups. Where values such as endpoints or resource identifiers are specific to a deployment, we use descriptive placeholders such as <RDS_ENDPOINT> that must be replaced with the actual values from the AWS Console.

Recipe #1: Creating AWS Instance and Managing Database Connection

Amazon RDS takes care of the heavy lifting of database infrastructure, such as hardware provisioning, patching, automated backups, and monitoring. We will now use RDS to host our PostgreSQL 18 instance in the cloud, connecting to it from both pgAdmin and an EC2-based psql session. The following architecture diagram shows the relationship between the components we will configure.

Configure RDS Instance

We begin by creating the RDS instance through the AWS Management Console. After logging in, we navigate to **RDS**, click **Create database**, and select **Standard Create** for full control over all options. We choose **PostgreSQL** as the engine and select version **18** from the version dropdown. For the deployment template, we choose **Production** to enable Multi-AZ deployment and automated backups by default. We supply a unique **DB instance identifier** such as **cookbook-pg18**, a master username, and a strong password.

We can now select an instance class appropriate for our workload, configure storage autoscaling, and ensure the instance sits inside a VPC that will also host our EC2 instance. For networking, we set **Public accessibility** to **No** so that the RDS instance is only reachable from within the VPC.
So here, we will now create a security group named **rds-pg18-sg** that permits inbound TCP traffic on port **5432** from the EC2 instance's security group only.

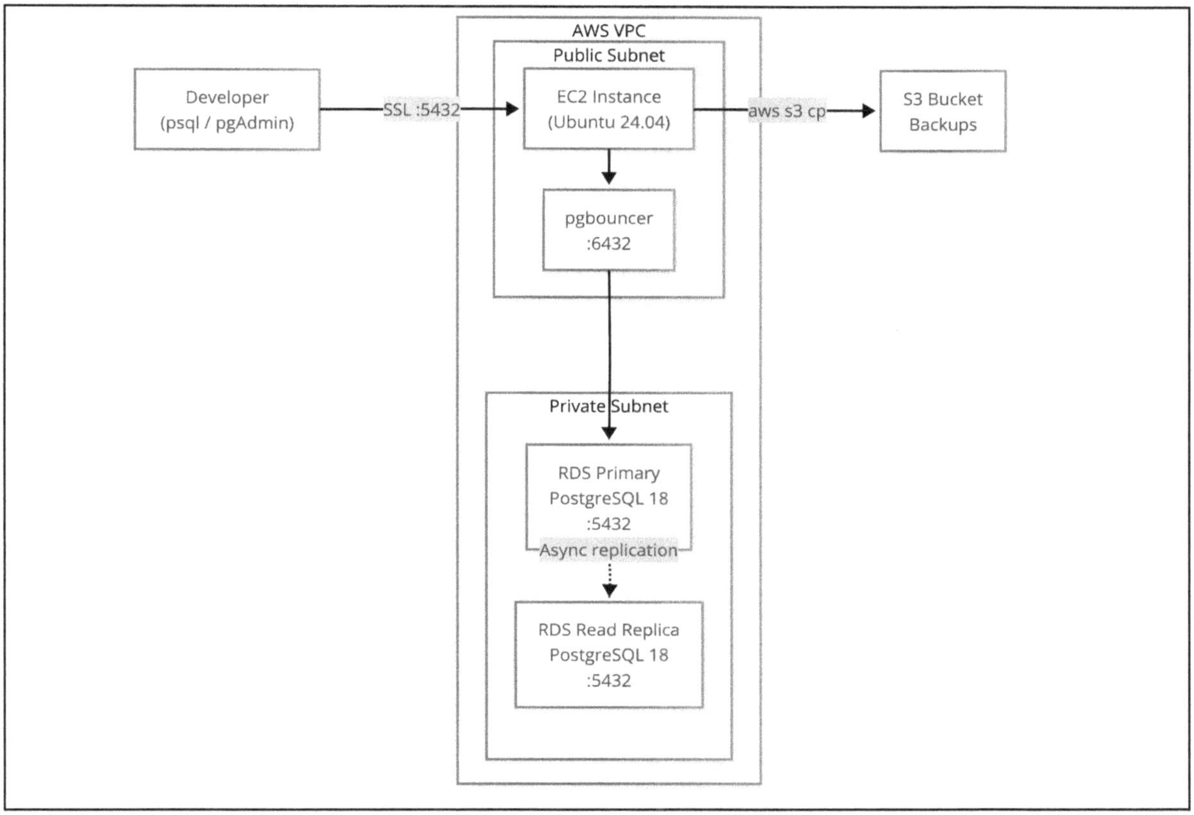

Fig 3.1: AWS Cloud Architecture: RDS + EC2 + VPC

This network isolation ensures that no external traffic can reach the database directly. We also enable storage encryption using AWS KMS and set the initial database name to **cookbook_db** to match our running sample application.

Once RDS instance reaches **Available** state in RDS Console, we note the endpoint hostname. It look like **cookbook-pg18.xxxxxxxx.us-east-1.rds.amazonaws.com**. We will use this value in place of **<RDS_ENDPOINT>** throughout every subsequent recipe in this chapter.

Launch and Connect EC2 Instance

We launch an Ubuntu 24.04 LTS EC2 instance in the same VPC as the RDS instance. We will now assign it a security group named **ec2-cookbook-sg** that permits inbound SSH on port **22** from our development machine's IP address. After the instance starts, we SSH into it and install the PostgreSQL 18 client tools.

At this point, we will run the following:

```
sudo apt update && sudo apt upgrade -y
```

```
sudo apt install -y curl ca-certificates
sudo install -d /usr/share/postgresql-common/pgdg
sudo curl -o /usr/share/postgresql-
common/pgdg/apt.postgresql.org.asc \
  --fail https://www.postgresql.org/media/keys/ACCC4CF8.asc
. /etc/os-release
sudo sh -c "echo 'deb [signed-by=/usr/share/postgresql-
common/pgdg/apt.postgresql.org.asc] \
  https://apt.postgresql.org/pub/repos/apt $VERSION_CODENAME-pgdg
main' \
  > /etc/apt/sources.list.d/pgdg.list"
sudo apt update
sudo apt install -y postgresql-client-18
```

In the following script, we will install only the client package here because the EC2 instance acts as a management host, not a database server. With the client installed, we test connectivity to the RDS instance from the EC2 machine. So, let us run the following command, substituting the actual RDS endpoint and master username:

```
psql --host=<RDS_ENDPOINT> --port=5432 \
     --username=<MASTER_USERNAME> \
     --password --dbname=cookbook_db
```

After entering the master password, the terminal connects to our RDS instance and presents the psql prompt, confirming end-to-end connectivity from the EC2 host to the managed PostgreSQL 18 cluster.

```
psql (18.0)
SSL connection (protocol: TLSv1.3, cipher: TLS_AES_256_GCM_SHA384,
bits: 256, compression: off)
Type "help" for help.
cookbook_db=>
```

The SSL line in the output confirms that our connection is encrypted in transit. All RDS instances enforce SSL by default, and PostgreSQL negotiates TLS 1.3 when both client and server support it. We exit psql with **\q** and proceed to import our schema into the cloud database.

To seed the RDS instance with the tables and data we created in Chapters 1 and 2, we dump the local **cookbook_db** database and restore it to the cloud. With this in mind, we will now run the following commands on the EC2 instance, after copying the dump file from our local machine via **scp**:

```
# Run this on our local machine first:
pg_dump --host=localhost --port=5432 --username=postgres \
        --format=custom --file=cookbook_db.dump cookbook_db

# Copy the dump to the EC2 instance:
scp -i <KEY_FILE>.pem cookbook_db.dump ubuntu@<EC2_PUBLIC_IP>:~/

# Now run this on the EC2 instance:
pg_restore --host=<RDS_ENDPOINT> --port=5432 \
           --username=<MASTER_USERNAME> --password \
           --dbname=cookbook_db --verbose ~/cookbook_db.dump
```

After the restore completes, we connect to the RDS instance and verify that our schemas, tables, and data are present. We refer to the schema structure we established in Chapter 2 for the list of objects we expect to find.

Recipe #2: Running Native Backup and Restore with EC2

Regular backups are the most fundamental safeguard for any production database. In this recipe, we use **pg_dump** from our EC2 instance to create a custom-format backup of our RDS-hosted **cookbook_db** database, store it in an S3 bucket for durable long-term retention, and then restore it to a recovery database using **pg_restore**.

Backup Database

We now proceed to create a directory on the EC2 instance to store our backup files, then run **pg_dump** against the RDS endpoint:

```
mkdir -p ~/cookbook_backups

pg_dump --host=<RDS_ENDPOINT> --port=5432 \
        --username=<MASTER_USERNAME> --password \
        --format=custom \
```

```
        --file=~/cookbook_backups/cookbook_db_$(date
+%Y%m%d_%H%M%S).dump \
        --dbname=cookbook_db
```

The **--format=custom** flag produces a compressed, binary dump that supports selective restoration by schema or table. The **$(date +%Y%m%d_%H%M%S)** suffix timestamps the file name, preventing overwrites and making it easy to identify which backup corresponds to a particular point in time.

We will now install the AWS CLI and upload the backup to S3 for durable long-term storage:

```
sudo apt install -y awscli
aws configure


# Create the S3 bucket (replace <YOUR_REGION> with your AWS
region):
aws s3api create-bucket \
    --bucket cookbook-db-backups \
    --region <YOUR_REGION> \
    --create-bucket-configuration LocationConstraint=<YOUR_REGION>


# Enable versioning for backup retention:
aws s3api put-bucket-versioning \
    --bucket cookbook-db-backups \
    --versioning-configuration Status=Enabled


# Upload the dump file:
aws s3 cp ~/cookbook_backups/cookbook_db_*.dump \
         s3://cookbook-db-backups/
```

Once we enable the bucket versioning, it then ensures that even if we accidentally upload a corrupt dump, previous versions remain retrievable. The AWS CLI confirms the upload with the S3 URI of the stored object. We can list the bucket contents at any time to audit available restore points.

Restore Database from Backup

To restore the database, we first create a recovery target database on the RDS instance and then use **pg_restore** to load the dump as shown below:

```
# Create the recovery database:
psql --host=<RDS_ENDPOINT> --port=5432 \
     --username=<MASTER_USERNAME> --password \
     --dbname=postgres \
     --command="CREATE DATABASE cookbook_db_restore;"

# Download the dump from S3:
aws s3 cp s3://cookbook-db-backups/<DUMP_FILENAME>
~/cookbook_backups/

# Restore into the recovery database:
pg_restore --host=<RDS_ENDPOINT> --port=5432 \
           --username=<MASTER_USERNAME> --password \
           --dbname=cookbook_db_restore \
           --verbose \
           ~/cookbook_backups/<DUMP_FILENAME>
```

After the restore finishes, we connect to **cookbook_db_restore** and confirm that our schemas and tables are intact. So here, we will then run the following verification queries:

```
psql --host=<RDS_ENDPOINT> --port=5432 \
     --username=<MASTER_USERNAME> --password \
     --dbname=cookbook_db_restore \
     --command="\dn; \dt hr.*; \dt sales.*; \dt production.*;"
```

The output lists all three schemas and their tables, confirming a successful restoration of every object we defined in Chapter 2. We drop the recovery database after verification to avoid unnecessary RDS storage charges.

Recipe #3: Running Native Backup and Restore with RDS

AWS RDS provides a built-in snapshot mechanism that operates at the storage layer, producing a point-in-time image of the entire DB instance without requiring us to run **pg_dump** manually. In this recipe, we configure automated backups, create a manual snapshot, and restore our

cookbook_db instance from that snapshot to a fresh RDS instance.

Create Manual Snapshot

We first verify that automated backups are enabled on the RDS instance, because manual snapshots depend on the backup infrastructure that automated backups set up. In the RDS Console, we select the **cookbook-pg18** instance, click **Modify**, scroll to the **Backup** section, and set the retention period to **7** days. We then apply the change immediately.

We then create a manual snapshot by selecting the RDS instance and choosing **Take snapshot** from the **Actions** menu. We supply a descriptive name such as **cookbook-pg18-manual-snap-1** and click **Take snapshot**. AWS transfers the instance storage state to S3, and the snapshot status transitions from **creating** to **available** within a few minutes for a small instance.

Restore from Snapshot and Verify

At this point, we navigate to the **Snapshots** section in the RDS Console and select our snapshot. We choose **Restore snapshot** from the **Actions** menu. Next, we configure the new instance as follows:

Parameter	Value
DB instance identifier	cookbook-pg18-restored
DB instance class	Same as source or downscaled for testing
Storage type	gp3
VPC	Same VPC as the source instance
Security group	rds-pg18-sg (reuse the existing group)
Database port	5432

After clicking **Restore DB Instance**, AWS creates a new instance from the snapshot storage. Once the restored instance reaches the **Available** state, we connect from the EC2 host and run a quick schema check to confirm data integrity:

```
psql --host=<RESTORED_RDS_ENDPOINT> --port=5432 \
     --username=<MASTER_USERNAME> --password \
     --dbname=cookbook_db \
     --command="SELECT count(*) FROM hr.employees;"
```

The row count must match the value from the source instance at snapshot time, confirming that the restored cluster is fully consistent. If we intend to use the restored instance as our primary cluster going forward, we update the application's connection string to point to the new endpoint. We will cover connection string management in detail in Recipe #4.

Recipe #4: Manage Database Connection on AWS

The management of database connections is as important as managing the database itself. Uncontrolled connection growth exhausts server memory, and direct application connections to RDS introduce unnecessary latency on every new request. In this recipe, we configure security group rules to control network access and deploy **pgbouncer** on the EC2 instance as a connection pool that sits between our application and the RDS cluster.

Modify Security Group Rules

We will then update the inbound rules of **rds-pg18-sg** so that only the EC2 instance can reach the RDS endpoint on port **5432**. In the AWS Console, we navigate to **EC2 > Security Groups**, select **rds-pg18-sg**, and edit the inbound rules to add the following entry:

Type	Protocol	Port Range	Source
PostgreSQL	TCP	5432	ec2-cookbook-sg (the EC2 security group ID)

This rule allows PostgreSQL traffic only from resources that belong to **ec2-cookbook-sg**, preventing any direct external access to the RDS endpoint. Applications that connect through pgbouncer on the EC2 instance benefit from this network topology because all pooled connections originate from the EC2 host, which already belongs to the permitted security group.

Install and Configure pgbouncer

Let us now install **pgbouncer** on the EC2 instance:

```
sudo apt install -y pgbouncer
```

We will now create a configuration directory and write the **pgbouncer.ini** file:

```
mkdir -p ~/pgbouncer


cat > ~/pgbouncer/pgbouncer.ini << 'EOF'
[databases]
cookbook_db = host=<RDS_ENDPOINT> port=5432 dbname=cookbook_db

[pgbouncer]
listen_addr         = *
listen_port         = 6432
auth_type           = scram-sha-256
```

```
auth_file              = /home/ubuntu/pgbouncer/users.txt
pool_mode              = transaction
max_client_conn        = 200
default_pool_size      = 20
logfile                = /var/log/pgbouncer/pgbouncer.log
pidfile                = /var/run/pgbouncer/pgbouncer.pid
admin_users            = <MASTER_USERNAME>
server_tls_sslmode     = require
EOF
```

The **auth_type = scram-sha-256** setting aligns with the PostgreSQL default that replaces the deprecated **md5** authentication method, as we covered in Chapter 1. The **pool_mode = transaction** setting returns server connections to the pool after each transaction completes, maximizing connection reuse. The **max_client_conn = 200** limit allows up to 200 concurrent application connections while maintaining only **default_pool_size = 20** persistent server-side connections to RDS.

In the following script, we will create the credentials file and start **pgbouncer** as a system service:

```
# Write the credentials file (replace placeholders):
echo '"<MASTER_USERNAME>" "<MASTER_PASSWORD>"' >
~/pgbouncer/users.txt
chmod 600 ~/pgbouncer/users.txt

# Create required directories:
sudo mkdir -p /var/log/pgbouncer /var/run/pgbouncer
sudo chown ubuntu:ubuntu /var/log/pgbouncer /var/run/pgbouncer

# Start pgbouncer:
pgbouncer -d ~/pgbouncer/pgbouncer.ini
```

With this in mind, we will now verify that **pgbouncer** is listening on port **6432** by connecting through the pool and querying the database:

```
psql --host=127.0.0.1 --port=6432 \
```

```
--username=<MASTER_USERNAME> --password \
--dbname=cookbook_db \
--command="SELECT count(*) FROM hr.employees;"
```

The query returns the same employee count as a direct connection, confirming that **pgbouncer** is proxying our connection transparently to RDS. The following diagram illustrates the connection flow through the pool.

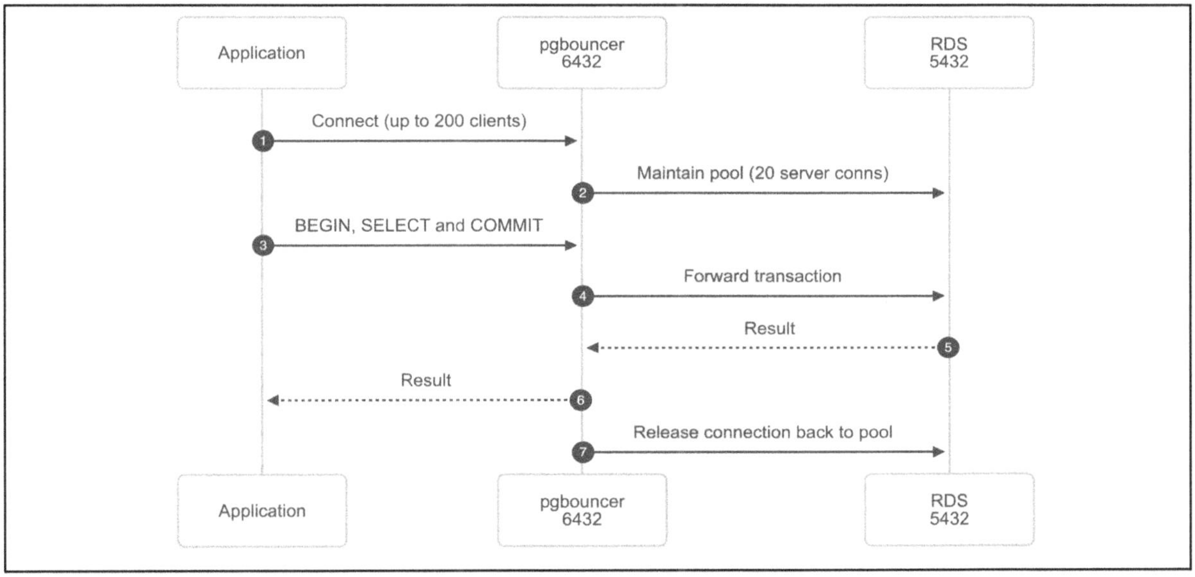

Fig 3.2: pgbouncer Connection Pooling Flow

Recipe #5: Performing Database Replication on AWS

AWS RDS read replicas allow us to offload read-heavy workloads from the primary instance, improving overall throughput and providing a warm standby that can be promoted in a disaster recovery scenario. In this recipe, we create a read replica of our **cookbook-pg18** instance, verify replication, and monitor replica lag.

Create Read Replica

Automatic backups must be enabled before RDS can create a read replica. We confirmed backup configuration in Recipe #3, so we proceed directly to replica creation. In the RDS Console, we select the **cookbook-pg18** instance, click **Actions**, and choose **Create read replica**. We provide the following configuration:

Parameter	Value
DB instance identifier	cookbook-pg18-replica

Destination Region	Same region as primary (us-east-1)
DB instance class	Same as or smaller than the primary
Storage type	gp3
Security group	rds-pg18-sg

After clicking **Create read replica**, AWS bootstraps the replica from the primary's latest automated backup and then streams WAL changes continuously to keep it current. We wait for the replica to reach the **Available** state, then connect to it and run a verification query:

```
psql --host=<READ_REPLICA_ENDPOINT> --port=5432 \
     --username=<MASTER_USERNAME> --password \
     --dbname=cookbook_db \
     --command="SELECT count(*) FROM hr.employees;"
```

The row count must match the primary. Any attempt to run a write operation on the replica produces an error because read replicas are strictly read-only, enforcing a clean separation of read and write workloads.

Monitor Replication Performance

Here, we will monitor replica lag using AWS Console's built-in **ReplicaLag** CloudWatch metric, and a direct query against the PostgreSQL system catalog on the replica.

We will now run the following SQL on the replica instance to observe its streaming replication state:

```
SELECT
    now() - pg_last_xact_replay_timestamp() AS replication_lag,
    pg_is_in_recovery()                      AS is_replica,
    pg_last_wal_receive_lsn()                AS last_received_lsn,
    pg_last_wal_replay_lsn()                 AS last_replayed_lsn;
```

The output shows the current replication lag as an interval, confirms that the instance is operating as a replica, and displays the WAL positions of the most recently received and replayed log segments. A lag close to zero seconds indicates a healthy, low-latency replication stream. If the lag grows persistently, we should review the replica instance's CPU and I/O capacity relative to the primary's write throughput.

```
 replication_lag | is_replica | last_received_lsn |
last_replayed_lsn
-----------------+------------+-------------------+-----------------
--
```

```
 00:00:00.234512 | t                  | 0/A1234B00            | 0/A1234B00
(1 row)
```

The sub-second lag in this output confirms that our replica is keeping pace with the primary's WAL stream. In the RDS Console, we can also navigate to the **`Monitoring`** tab for the replica instance and observe the **`ReplicaLag`** CloudWatch metric over time, which provides historical visibility into lag trends.

Recipe #6: Running Bi-directional Replication

Bi-directional replication allows two PostgreSQL instances to act as both a publisher and a subscriber simultaneously, so that writes on either node propagate to the other. This pattern supports multi-region active-active deployments and distributed workloads. From here, we use the **`pglogical`** extension, which implements logical replication at the publication layer, enabling selective table inclusion and schema-level control that physical streaming replication does not provide. The following diagram shows the bi-directional flow.

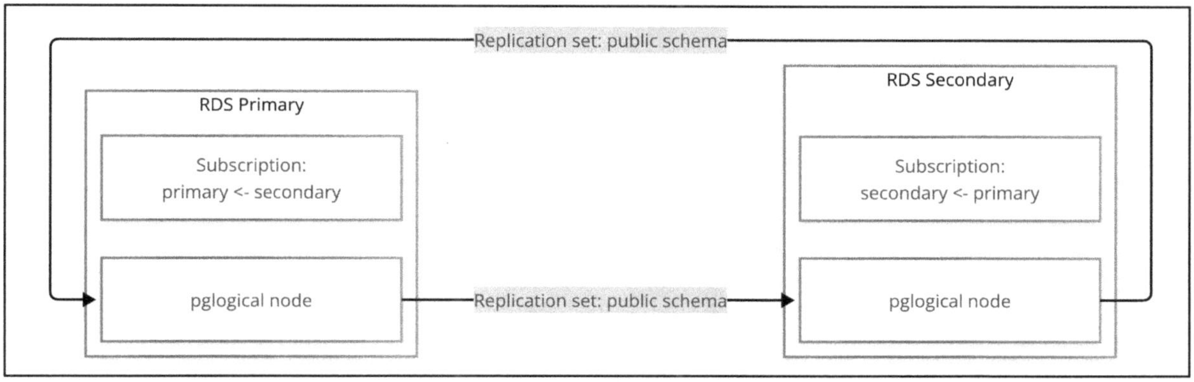

Fig 3.3: pglogical Bi-directional Replication Topology

Enable pglogical on RDS Instances

We proceed to enable **`pglogical`** by modifying the parameter group for both RDS instances. In the RDS Console, we create a custom parameter group based on the **`postgres18`** family if one does not already exist, then set the following parameters:

Parameter	**Value**	**Purpose**
shared_preload_libraries	pglogical	Load the extension at startup
rds.logical_replication	1	Enable logical WAL level on RDS
wal_level	logical	Auto-set when rds.logical_replication = 1
max_replication_slots	10	Allow enough slots for subscriptions
max_wal_senders	10	Allow enough WAL sender processes

So here, we will then apply the parameter group to both the primary and secondary RDS instances and reboot each instance to pick up the **shared_preload_libraries** change. After the reboots complete, we connect to each instance and install the extension. We will then run the following SQL on both instances:

```
CREATE EXTENSION pglogical;
```

Configure Replication Nodes

Each instance requires a unique **pglogical** node definition that identifies it within the replication topology.

In the following, we will run the following SQL on the primary instance:

```
-- Run on the PRIMARY instance:
SELECT pglogical.create_node(
    node_name := 'cookbook_primary',
    dsn       := 'host=<PRIMARY_RDS_ENDPOINT> port=5432
                  dbname=cookbook_db
                  user=<MASTER_USERNAME>
                  password=<MASTER_PASSWORD>'
);

-- Add all tables in the public, hr, sales, and production schemas:
SELECT pglogical.replication_set_add_all_tables('default',
ARRAY['public','hr','sales','production']);
SELECT pglogical.replication_set_add_all_sequences('default',
ARRAY['public','hr','sales','production']);
```

We then run the equivalent node creation on the secondary instance. We will now run the following SQL on the secondary instance:

```
-- Run on the SECONDARY instance:
SELECT pglogical.create_node(
    node_name := 'cookbook_secondary',
    dsn       := 'host=<SECONDARY_RDS_ENDPOINT> port=5432
                  dbname=cookbook_db
```

```
                    user=<MASTER_USERNAME>
                    password=<MASTER_PASSWORD>'
);

SELECT pglogical.replication_set_add_all_tables('default',
ARRAY['public','hr','sales','production']);
SELECT pglogical.replication_set_add_all_sequences('default',
ARRAY['public','hr','sales','production']);
```

Create Replication Subscriptions

Bi-directional replication requires a subscription on each node pointing to the other node. We first create the subscription on the secondary instance that pulls changes from the primary. At this point, we will run the following SQL on the secondary instance:

```
-- Run on the SECONDARY instance:
SELECT pglogical.create_subscription(
    subscription_name   := 'sub_primary_to_secondary',
    provider_dsn        := 'host=<PRIMARY_RDS_ENDPOINT> port=5432
                            dbname=cookbook_db
                            user=<MASTER_USERNAME>
                            password=<MASTER_PASSWORD>',
    replication_sets    := ARRAY['default'],
    synchronize_structure := false,
    synchronize_data      := true
);
```

We then create the reverse subscription on the primary instance, completing the bi-directional loop. In the following SQL block, we will on the primary instance:

```
-- Run on the PRIMARY instance:
SELECT pglogical.create_subscription(
    subscription_name   := 'sub_secondary_to_primary',
    provider_dsn        := 'host=<SECONDARY_RDS_ENDPOINT> port=5432
                            dbname=cookbook_db
```

```
                         user=<MASTER_USERNAME>
                         password=<MASTER_PASSWORD>',
    replication_sets    := ARRAY['default'],
    synchronize_structure := false,
    synchronize_data      := true
);
```

So, let us verify that both subscriptions are actively replicating by running the following SQL on each instance:

```
SELECT * FROM pglogical.show_subscription_status();
```

The output must show a **status** of **replicating** for each subscription. To confirm that changes actually flow between instances, we insert a test row into **hr.employees** on the primary and verify its presence on the secondary. With this in mind, we will now run the following SQL on the primary instance:

```
-- On the PRIMARY:
INSERT INTO hr.employees (first_name, last_name, email, department, salary)
VALUES ('Cloud', 'TestUser', 'cloud.test@techparts.io', 'Engineering', 91000.00);

-- On the SECONDARY (verify replication):
SELECT employee_id, first_name, last_name
FROM hr.employees
WHERE email = 'cloud.test@techparts.io';
```

The row appears on the secondary within milliseconds, confirming that the **pglogical** pipeline is operational. If replication issues arise, we review the PostgreSQL logs in the RDS Console under the **Logs & events** tab for each instance, looking for errors related to **pglogical** worker processes or replication slot activity. Common causes include insufficient **max_replication_slots** values, network security group misconfigurations, or mismatched schema structures between the two instances.

Summary

This chapter extended our **cookbook_db** sample application into the cloud by provisioning a

PostgreSQL instance on Amazon RDS, connecting to it from an EC2 host, and importing the schema and data we built in Chapters 1 and 2. We performed both native **pg_dump** backups with S3 storage and RDS snapshot-based backups, giving us a file-level backup for selective restoration and a storage-layer snapshot for full instance recovery.

We secured and optimized connectivity by locking down the RDS security group to EC2-only access and deploying **pgbouncer** in transaction pooling mode, which allows up to 200 application connections to share just 20 persistent server-side connections. This dramatically reduces the per-connection overhead on the RDS instance and improves scalability without requiring any changes to application code. We then implemented RDS read replica for read scale-out and disaster recovery promotion, and a bi-directional logical replication setup using **pglogical** that synchronizes writes between two independent PostgreSQL 18 instances.

CHAPTER 4
DATABASE MIGRATION TO CLOUD AND POSTGRESQL

Introduction

This chapter walks us through a range of database migration techniques that take our **cookbook_db** sample application from an on-premises host into a cloud-hosted PostgreSQL 18 environment, and also covers how to consolidate data from other database engines into PostgreSQL. We will migrate from an on-premises server to an AWS EC2 or RDS instance using native **pg_dump** and **pg_restore** flows, orchestrate a managed migration using AWS Data Migration Service (DMS), move from an EC2-hosted cluster to a managed RDS instance, and use **pgloader** to bring data in from MySQL. We will also configure Foreign Data Wrappers to query remote MySQL tables directly from PostgreSQL.

Beyond these familiar patterns, this edition provides a new recipe dedicated to upgrading an existing cluster to PostgreSQL 18 using **pg_upgrade**. This release introduces several operationally significant improvements, like the utility preserves optimizer statistics across a major version upgrade, runs its database compatibility checks in parallel, and offers a new **--swap** mode that exchanges data directories rather than copying or linking files. We will walk through the full upgrade flow including the **--check** dry run, the checksum compatibility considerations introduced in Chapter 1, and the post-upgrade validation steps that confirm the upgraded cluster is production ready.

Recipe #1: Migrating to AWS EC2/RDS Instance

This recipe moves our running **cookbook_db** database from an on-premises Ubuntu server to the AWS EC2 or RDS instance we provisioned in Chapter 3. We will create a compressed tar archive of the source database, transfer it securely into the AWS environment, restore it against the cloud target, and finally verify that every schema and table arrived intact. Because we established the RDS endpoint, EC2 host, and the network layout in Chapter 3, we can focus here purely on the migration mechanics rather than infrastructure provisioning.

Create Database Backup

We begin on the on-premises PostgreSQL server where **cookbook_db** is currently running. We now proceed to confirm the service is active and that we have credentials for a role with sufficient privileges to dump every schema. We then run **pg_dump** to produce a tar-format archive. The tar format supports selective restoration of individual schemas and tables later, which is useful when only parts of the source need to be migrated.

At this stage, we will then run the following command from the on-premises host:

```
pg_dump -U <USERNAME> -W -F t \
        -f cookbook_db_backup.tar cookbook_db
```

We enter the role password when prompted. The **-F t** flag requests tar output, **-f** names the destination file, and **-W** forces an explicit password prompt.

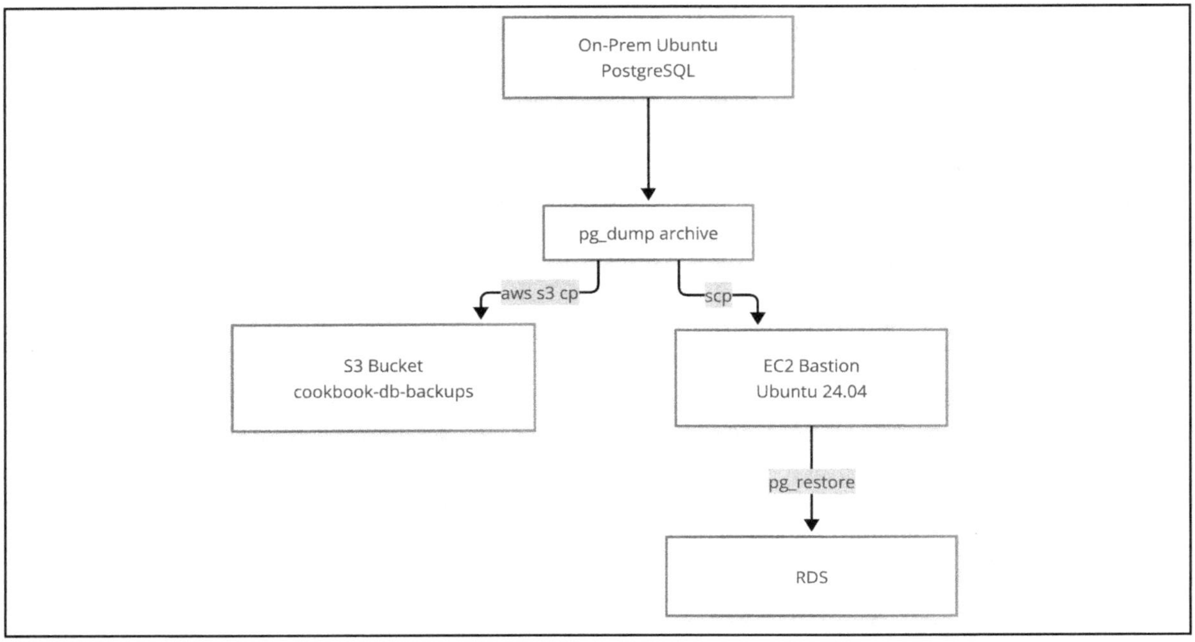

Fig 4.1: On-Premises to AWS Migration Flow

The resulting archive contains every table, index, sequence, view, function, and extension that we created across Chapters 1 and 2, including the temporal constraint objects and virtual generated columns we added to **hr.employees** and **hr.project_assignments**. We can verify the archive by listing its table-of-contents before transferring it.

Transfer Backup to AWS Environment

For an EC2 target, we use **scp** to copy the tar file directly into the home directory of the EC2 bastion we established in Chapter 3. Here, we will run the following command from the on-premises host:

```
scp -i <PATH_TO_PRIVATE_KEY> cookbook_db_backup.tar \
    ubuntu@<EC2_PUBLIC_DNS>:/home/ubuntu/
```

For an RDS target, we instead upload the archive to the S3 bucket we created in Chapter 3, because RDS itself cannot accept direct file transfers. We can now run the following command from the EC2 bastion after copying the file over with **scp**, or directly from the on-premises host if the AWS CLI is configured there:

```
aws s3 cp cookbook_db_backup.tar \
```

```
        s3://cookbook-db-backups/migration/
```

When we stage the archive in S3, it gives us a durable intermediate location that survives restarts of the EC2 bastion and acts as a recovery point during the migration itself. If the restore fails, we can always re-download the same archive and retry without having to regenerate it from the source database. We proceed to the verification and restoration step only after confirming the upload completed successfully by running **aws s3 ls s3://cookbook-db-backups/migration/** and observing the expected file size.

Verify Migration

For the EC2 target, we first create an empty target database on the EC2-hosted PostgreSQL cluster and then restore the archive. We covered the installation of the PostgreSQL 18 client and server packages in Chapter 1 and Chapter 3, so we refer back to those chapters for the setup steps. So here, we will then run the following commands on the EC2 host:

```
createdb -U <USERNAME> -W cookbook_db


pg_restore -U <USERNAME> -W \
           -d cookbook_db \
           /home/ubuntu/cookbook_db_backup.tar
```

For the RDS target, we create the empty database via **psql** against the managed endpoint, then restore the archive directly from the EC2 bastion where it was downloaded from S3:

```
psql --host=<RDS_ENDPOINT> --port=5432 \
     --username=<MASTER_USERNAME> --password \
     --dbname=postgres \
     --command="CREATE DATABASE cookbook_db;"


pg_restore -h <RDS_ENDPOINT> \
           -U <MASTER_USERNAME> -W \
           -d cookbook_db \
           cookbook_db_backup.tar
```

After the restore finishes, we verify the migration by connecting to the target and running a series of SQL queries that confirm every expected object is present and populated.

```
\dn
```

```
\dt hr.*
\dt sales.*
\dt production.*
SELECT count(*) FROM hr.employees;
SELECT count(*) FROM hr.project_assignments;
SELECT count(*) FROM sales.orders;
```

The schema listing must display **public**, **hr**, **sales**, and **production** schemas, and the row counts must match the source. A row-count mismatch indicates an incomplete dump or restore and requires investigation before we decommission the on-premises instance. With verification complete, we have successfully lifted the **cookbook_db** database into its cloud home.

Recipe #2: Utilizing AWS Data Migration Service (DMS)

AWS Data Migration Service orchestrates a managed migration between a source and target database with minimal downtime. Unlike the dump-and-restore pattern in Recipe #1, DMS can continue replicating changes from the source database while the initial bulk load is in progress, enabling near-zero downtime cutovers. In this recipe, we use DMS to move our **cookbook_db** from an on-premises PostgreSQL server to the PostgreSQL 18 RDS instance we provisioned in Chapter 3.

Setup AWS Environment

At this stage, we confirm that the on-premises PostgreSQL server is reachable from the AWS VPC where our RDS instance resides. If the on-premises host sits in a different AWS account or VPC, we create a VPC peering connection so that DMS replication instances can reach both endpoints.

In the AWS Management Console, we navigate to the VPC Dashboard, select **Peering Connections**, and create a new connection specifying the requester and accepter VPC identifiers. We accept the connection from the peer side and update both route tables to add entries for the opposite CIDR block. Once the peering is active and route tables are updated, DMS traffic can flow in both directions.

We also configure the on-premises PostgreSQL server for logical replication by setting **wal_level = logical** in **postgresql.conf**, increasing **max_replication_slots** and **max_wal_senders** to at least **10**, and adding an entry to **pg_hba.conf** that permits replication connections from the DMS replication instance's IP range. We restart the on-premises cluster to apply these changes before proceeding. DMS requires this configuration to perform the ongoing change data capture that makes near-zero downtime cutovers possible.

Create DMS Replication Instance and Endpoints

In the AWS Management Console, we navigate to the DMS Dashboard and click **Replication instances**. So here, we create a new replication instance named **cookbook-migration-ri** with an instance class appropriate for our dataset size, allocated storage of at least **50 GB**, and the VPC and subnets that host our RDS target. The replication instance is the compute engine that reads from the source, buffers changes, and applies them to the target, so its network reachability to both endpoints is essential.

After creation, we confirm the instance reaches the **available** state before creating endpoints. We will then create two endpoints, one for the source and one for the target. In the DMS Dashboard, we click **Endpoints** and create the following two configurations. The source endpoint points to the on-premises server and the target endpoint points to the RDS instance we prepared in Chapter 3.

Parameter	Source Endpoint	Target Endpoint
Endpoint identifier	cookbook-src-onprem	cookbook-tgt-rds-pg18
Endpoint type	Source	Target
Engine	PostgreSQL	PostgreSQL
Server name	on-premises hostname	<RDS_ENDPOINT>
Port	5432	5432
SSL mode	require	require
Database name	cookbook_db	cookbook_db

After creating both endpoints, we test each connection from within the DMS Dashboard by selecting the endpoint and clicking **Test endpoint connection**. Both tests must succeed before moving on. A failure here almost always indicates a security group rule that blocks traffic between the replication instance and the endpoint, or an authentication issue in **pg_hba.conf** on the source. We resolve any failures before creating the migration task itself.

Create and Monitor Migration Task

In the DMS Dashboard, we click **Database migration tasks** and create a new task named **cookbook-db-migration**. With this in place, we select the replication instance we created, attach both endpoints, and choose **Migrate existing data and replicate ongoing changes** as the migration type. This mode performs a full load of the current state followed by continuous replication of new changes.

We now proceed to configure logging at the **INFO** level and define table mappings that include every schema in **cookbook_db**, which means **public**, **hr**, **sales**, and **production**. We click **Create task** and monitor its progress in the DMS Dashboard. The task transitions through **Starting**, **Running** (full load), and finally **Load complete, replication ongoing** once every table has been copied. At this point, new writes against the on-premises database continue to propagate to the RDS target with only a small replication lag. When we are ready to cut over, we pause application writes against the on-premises source, wait for DMS to drain the remaining change queue, and then repoint application connection strings to the RDS endpoint.

This approach minimizes downtime to the drain window, which is typically seconds for small to medium workloads.

Recipe #3: Migrating Database from EC2 to RDS Instance

When we run PostgreSQL on EC2, it gives us full control over the operating system and database configuration. However, it also means we own the responsibility for patching, backups, high availability, and monitoring. The migration to RDS offloads that operational burden to AWS in exchange for slightly less configuration flexibility. In this recipe, we move **cookbook_db** from an EC2-hosted cluster to a managed RDS instance using an S3-based restore workflow that takes advantage of the **aws rds restore-db-instance-from-s3** command.

Create Backup and Upload to S3

On the EC2 instance hosting our current PostgreSQL cluster, we run **pg_dump** to produce a tar archive of **cookbook_db**. We then upload it to the S3 bucket from Chapter 3:

```
pg_dump -U <USERNAME> -W -F t \
        -f cookbook_db_backup.tar cookbook_db


aws s3 cp cookbook_db_backup.tar \
          s3://cookbook-db-backups/ec2-to-rds/
```

We then create an IAM role that grants the target RDS service permission to read the backup object from S3. In the IAM Dashboard, we create a new role for the RDS service, attach the **AmazonS3ReadOnlyAccess** managed policy (or a custom policy scoped to the specific bucket for tighter security), and record the role ARN. We associate this role with the new RDS instance during creation so that the restore operation can fetch the backup automatically. This IAM-based approach avoids embedding any AWS credentials in scripts or configuration files.

Restore Database to RDS

At this point, we will create an empty target database on the new RDS instance and then trigger the S3-based restore using the AWS CLI. In the following command, we will from any host with the AWS CLI configured:

```
aws rds restore-db-instance-from-s3 \
```

```
--db-instance-identifier cookbook-pg18-from-s3 \
--db-instance-class db.t3.medium \
--engine postgres \
--engine-version 18.0 \
--master-username <MASTER_USERNAME> \
--master-user-password <MASTER_USER_PASSWORD> \
--vpc-security-group-ids <VPC_SECURITY_GROUP_ID> \
--s3-bucket-name cookbook-db-backups \
--s3-prefix ec2-to-rds/cookbook_db_backup.tar \
--s3-ingestion-role-arn <IAM_ROLE_ARN> \
--source-engine postgres \
--source-engine-version 18.0 \
--region <AWS_REGION> \
--availability-zone <AVAILABILITY_ZONE> \
--backup-retention-period 7
```

AWS provisions the new RDS instance, pulls the backup object from S3, and restores it into the managed service. The whole operation typically takes a few minutes for small databases and scales roughly linearly with archive size. Once the instance reaches the **available** state, we connect to it and run the same verification queries we used in Recipe #1 to confirm that every schema and table arrived intact, including the temporal constraints and virtual generated columns we configured in Chapter 2.

Monitor and Optimize

After the migration completes, we take advantage of the managed features that motivated the move. Here, we will enable enhanced monitoring in the RDS Console to capture per-second OS metrics, configure CloudWatch alarms on **CPUUtilization**, **FreeStorageSpace**, and **DatabaseConnections**, and review the **Performance Insights** dashboard to identify hot queries. If workload patterns suggest that the instance is undersized, we scale vertically by modifying the instance class.

We also revisit the configuration parameters we covered in Chapter 1 to verify that **shared_buffers**, **effective_cache_size**, and **maintenance_work_mem** are aligned with the managed instance class capacity.

Recipe #4: Preparing Pgloader

The **pgloader** utility is a powerful open-source tool that migrates data into PostgreSQL from a wide variety of source engines including MySQL, SQL Server, SQLite, and CSV files. It handles schema conversion, data type casting, and bulk loading in a single declarative command file. In this recipe, we install **pgloader** on our EC2 bastion host and prepare a generic command file template that we will customize for specific source engines in Recipe #5.

Install pgloader

On the Ubuntu 24.04 EC2 bastion we configured in Chapter 3, we install **pgloader** from the default package repository:

```
sudo apt update
sudo apt install -y pgloader
```

With this in mind, we will now verify the installation succeeded by checking the version:

```
pgloader --version
```

The terminal displays the version string and build timestamp, confirming that **pgloader** is on the PATH and ready for use. If the command is not found, we refer back to the package manager output to confirm the package installed without errors. At this point the tool is installed but not yet configured for any specific migration; the command file that we build next defines the source connection, the target connection, and the transformation rules.

Create pgloader Command file

At this stage, we will then confirm that both the source database (whether MySQL, SQL Server, or SQLite) and our target PostgreSQL cluster are running and reachable from the EC2 bastion, and that we have credentials for both. We then create a generic command file template that we will specialize in Recipe #5.

Here, we will run the following command to open a new command file:

```
nano pgloader_template.load
```

We can now add the following template content. Every placeholder enclosed in angle brackets must be replaced with real values before the command is executed:

```
LOAD DATABASE
    FROM <SOURCE_DB_CONNECTION_STRING>
    INTO <TARGET_DB_CONNECTION_STRING>
```

```
WITH include drop, create tables, create indexes,
     reset sequences, data only

SET maintenance_work_mem to '128MB',
    work_mem to '12MB',
    search_path to 'public'

CAST type <SOURCE_TYPE> to <TARGET_TYPE> drop typemod

BEFORE LOAD DO
$$ create schema if not exists public; $$;
```

The **WITH** clause instructs **pgloader** to drop existing target tables, recreate them from the source schema, rebuild indexes, and reset sequence values to match the source. The **SET** clause tunes session-level memory parameters to accelerate the bulk load. The **CAST** clause declares custom type conversions between source and target engines. The **BEFORE LOAD** block runs arbitrary SQL against the target before the load begins, which is useful to confirm that the schemas and extensions exist. We will now execute the command file by running **pgloader pgloader_template.load** once the placeholders are filled in.

Recipe #5: Migrating from MySQL to PostgreSQL

In this recipe, we migrate a MySQL database into our PostgreSQL cluster using the **pgloader** toolchain we prepared in Recipe #4. MySQL and PostgreSQL differ in several important ways, including how they represent dates, booleans, and small integers, so the command file must include explicit type casts to ensure the migrated data behaves correctly in the target. For this worked example, we assume a MySQL database named **legacy_sales** that contains historical transaction data we want to consolidate into the **sales** schema of our **cookbook_db** cluster.

Create pgloader Command file

So here, we will then confirm the MySQL server is reachable from the EC2 bastion, the MySQL credentials work, and that the target PostgreSQL cluster is accepting connections on its endpoint. We then create a dedicated command file for the MySQL migration:

```
nano mysql_to_postgresql.load
```

Let us now add the following content. The connection strings use standard URI format for both engines, and the **CAST** block handles the three most common MySQL-to-PostgreSQL type incompatibilities:

```
LOAD DATABASE
    FROM
mysql://<MYSQL_USER>:<MYSQL_PASSWORD>@<MYSQL_HOST>:3306/legacy_sale
s
    INTO
postgresql://<PG_USER>:<PG_PASSWORD>@<RDS_ENDPOINT>:5432/cookbook_d
b

WITH include drop, create tables, create indexes,
     reset sequences, data only

SET maintenance_work_mem to '128MB',
    work_mem to '12MB',
    search_path to 'sales'

CAST type datetime to timestamptz drop typemod,
     type date drop not null using zero-dates-to-null,
     type tinyint to smallint

BEFORE LOAD DO
$$ create schema if not exists sales; $$;
```

The **datetime to timestamptz** cast converts MySQL's naive datetime values into PostgreSQL's timezone-aware **timestamptz** type, preserving temporal accuracy. The **zero-dates-to-null** rule addresses MySQL's tolerance for invalid **'0000-00-00'** date values by converting them to SQL NULL, which PostgreSQL's stricter type system requires. The **tinyint to smallint** cast bridges MySQL's one-byte integer type to PostgreSQL's smallest native integer. Without these explicit casts the load would fail on the first row that trips a type incompatibility.

Run Migration

We will now execute the command file. At this point, we will run the following command from the EC2 bastion:

```
pgloader mysql_to_postgresql.load
```

The terminal streams progress messages including the number of rows read from the source and the number inserted into the target for each table. A successful run ends with a summary table showing zero errors and a per-table row count that matches the source. We then connect to the PostgreSQL cluster and run verification queries against the newly populated tables under the **sales** schema.

If any table reports errors, the log file captures the failing row and the specific cast that could not be applied, which we use to adjust the **CAST** block and retry the load.

```
2026-04-24T10:14:22.198000Z LOG pgloader version "3.6.10"
2026-04-24T10:14:22.210000Z LOG Data errors in '/tmp/pgloader/'
2026-04-24T10:14:22.211000Z LOG Parsing commands from file
"mysql_to_postgresql.load"


             table name     errors       rows      bytes      total
time
-----------------------  ---------  ---------  ---------  ---------
-----
 legacy_sales.customers          0     14,203     1.7 MB
2.112s
    legacy_sales.orders          0     87,441     9.4 MB
11.880s
legacy_sales.order_item          0    231,708    19.3 MB
24.506s
-----------------------  ---------  ---------  ---------  ---------
-----
                  Total          0    333,352    30.4 MB
38.498s
```

Recipe #6: Setting up Foreign Data Wrapper (FDW)

A Foreign Data Wrapper (FDW) enables a PostgreSQL server to query tables in a remote database as if they were local. Instead of physically migrating data, an FDW exposes the remote tables through the PostgreSQL catalog so that **SELECT**, and in some cases **INSERT** and **UPDATE**, work seamlessly across engines. In this recipe, we install the MySQL FDW, create a foreign server and user mapping, and define a foreign table that references a remote MySQL table.

We can now use this as a temporary integration bridge while preparing for a full **pgloader** migration, or as a permanent arrangement when the remote data must remain in its original system.

Install MySQL FDW

In the following script, we will install the MySQL FDW extension package for PostgreSQL 18 along with the MySQL client library that the extension depends on. So, let us run the following commands on the PostgreSQL host:

```
sudo apt install -y postgresql-18-mysql-fdw \
                     libmysqlclient-dev
```

We then enable the extension in the target database and define the foreign server that points to the remote MySQL instance. With this in mind, we will now run the following SQL inside **cookbook_db**:

```
CREATE EXTENSION mysql_fdw;


CREATE SERVER mysql_legacy
    FOREIGN DATA WRAPPER mysql_fdw
    OPTIONS (host 'mysql.internal.example.com', port '3306');


CREATE USER MAPPING FOR postgres
    SERVER mysql_legacy
    OPTIONS (username '<MYSQL_USER>', password '<MYSQL_PASSWORD>');
```

The **CREATE SERVER** statement registers the remote MySQL host under a local alias, and the **CREATE USER MAPPING** statement associates a local PostgreSQL role with MySQL credentials. Anyone connected as the **postgres** role can now access the remote MySQL server, subject to both PostgreSQL's grants and MySQL's own privilege model. In production, we would create a dedicated, minimally privileged PostgreSQL role for this mapping rather than using **postgres** directly, and we would store credentials in a secrets manager rather than embedding them in SQL scripts.

Create FDW Table

We now proceed to define a foreign table that maps to the remote MySQL **sales.orders_legacy** table. The column definitions must match the MySQL schema both in name and compatible data type.

Following is the quick query:

```
CREATE FOREIGN TABLE sales.orders_legacy (
    legacy_order_id     integer,
    order_date          timestamptz,
    customer_reference  varchar(50),
    subtotal            numeric(12,2),
    tax_amount          numeric(12,2),
    total_due           numeric(12,2),
    notes               text
)
SERVER mysql_legacy
OPTIONS (dbname 'legacy_sales', table_name 'orders');
```

We can now query the foreign table as if it were local. Here, we will run the following SQL to preview the remote data and then bulk-insert it into a native PostgreSQL table when we are satisfied with the result:

```
SELECT legacy_order_id, order_date, total_due
FROM   sales.orders_legacy
WHERE  order_date >= '2024-01-01'
ORDER  BY order_date DESC
LIMIT  10;


-- Bulk-migrate selected rows into the native orders table:
INSERT INTO sales.orders (customer_name, order_date, total_due,
territory)
SELECT customer_reference, order_date, total_due, 'Legacy'
FROM   sales.orders_legacy
WHERE  order_date >= '2024-01-01';
```

The **`INSERT ... SELECT`** pattern is especially useful during phased migrations where we move data in batches while application traffic still hits the legacy system. Once the foreign table is no longer needed, we drop it with **`DROP FOREIGN TABLE sales.orders_legacy`**. We then drop the user mapping and server objects when the MySQL backend is fully decommissioned, keeping the PostgreSQL catalog clean.

Recipe #7: Upgrading to PostgreSQL 18

Of all the migration scenarios covered in this chapter, the most common in practice is upgrading an existing PostgreSQL cluster to a newer major version. The **pg_upgrade** utility performs in-place major version upgrades by migrating system catalogs while leaving user data files in place, which is dramatically faster than a dump-and-restore for large databases.

In this recipe, we walk through a complete **pg_upgrade** from a PostgreSQL 16 cluster to a new PostgreSQL 18 cluster.

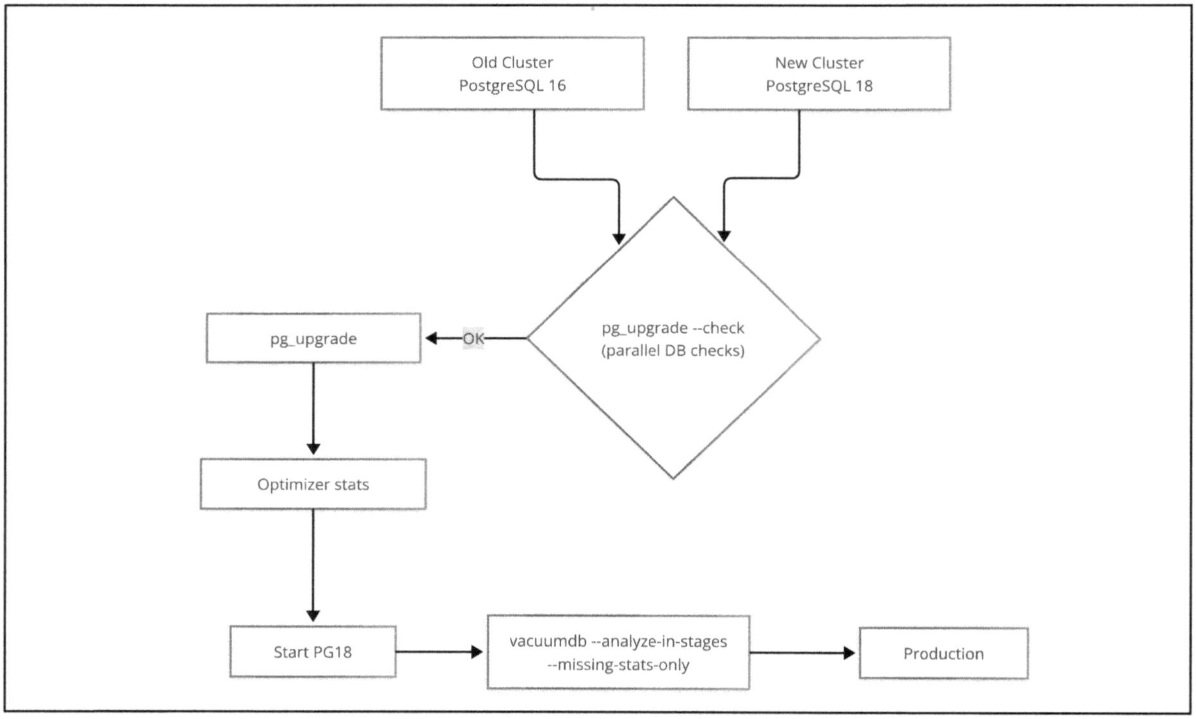

Fig 4.2: pg_upgrade Workflow

Preparing Old and New Clusters

We begin by installing PostgreSQL 18 alongside the existing PostgreSQL 16 cluster, using the installation steps we covered in Chapter 1. Both binary sets must be present on the host because **pg_upgrade** invokes the old cluster's binaries to read catalogs and the new cluster's binaries to write them.

Let us now initialize an empty data directory for the new cluster while taking care to match the checksum setting of the source. Because PostgreSQL 18 enables data checksums by default at

initdb (as we covered in Chapter 1) and the old PostgreSQL 16 cluster very likely does not have checksums enabled, we must either match the old setting or enable checksums on the old cluster before upgrading. We can now check the checksum status of the old cluster and initialize the new one to match.

So here, we will then run the following:

```
# Check the source cluster's checksum setting:
sudo -u postgres /usr/lib/postgresql/16/bin/pg_controldata \
     /var/lib/postgresql/16/main | grep "Data page checksum"

# If checksums are DISABLED on PG16, initialize PG18 without them:
sudo -u postgres /usr/lib/postgresql/18/bin/initdb \
     --no-data-checksums \
     -D /var/lib/postgresql/18/main

# Alternatively, enable checksums on the PG16 cluster first:
# sudo systemctl stop postgresql@16-main
# sudo -u postgres /usr/lib/postgresql/16/bin/pg_checksums \
#      --enable -D /var/lib/postgresql/16/main
```

If we want the upgraded cluster to benefit from the PostgreSQL default of enabling checksums, we run **pg_checksums --enable** on the stopped old cluster before the upgrade and then initialize the new cluster normally. That approach costs a one-time full table scan on the old cluster but produces a new cluster with full data integrity protection from the moment it starts.

For large production databases, this is typically the preferred path; for development or test upgrades where speed matters more than integrity guarantees, **--no-data-checksums** on the new cluster is the faster option.

Running Upgrade Compatibility Check

Before performing the actual upgrade, we run **pg_upgrade --check** in dry-run mode to identify any compatibility issues that would cause the real upgrade to fail. PostgreSQL 18's **pg_upgrade** runs these database-level checks in parallel when the **--jobs** option is specified, which dramatically reduces check time on clusters with many databases. We will then stop the old cluster first because **pg_upgrade** requires exclusive access to both data directories.

Let us now run the following commands:

```
# Stop the old cluster:
sudo systemctl stop postgresql@16-main

# Run the compatibility check as the postgres user:
sudo -u postgres /usr/lib/postgresql/18/bin/pg_upgrade \
     --old-datadir=/var/lib/postgresql/16/main \
     --new-datadir=/var/lib/postgresql/18/main \
     --old-bindir=/usr/lib/postgresql/16/bin \
     --new-bindir=/usr/lib/postgresql/18/bin \
     --jobs=4 \
     --check
```

The **`--check`** flag runs every compatibility validation without modifying either cluster. The **`--jobs=4`** flag parallelizes the checks across four worker processes, which is new in PostgreSQL 18. On a cluster with dozens of databases, this can reduce check time from minutes to seconds.

Here, a successful check will end with a following message:

```
Performing Consistency Checks
-----------------------------
Checking cluster versions                                      ok
Checking database user is the install user                     ok
Checking database connection settings                          ok
Checking for prepared transactions                             ok
Checking for contrib/isn with bigint-passing mismatch          ok
Checking data type usage                                       ok

*Clusters are compatible*
```

Any **`failed`** check must be resolved before proceeding. Typical blockers include prepared transactions left open in the old cluster (resolved by committing or rolling them back), incompatible extensions that lack a PostgreSQL 18 build (resolved by upgrading or removing the extension), and data type usage that has been deprecated (resolved by altering the affected tables). The check output identifies the specific object and schema for every problem it detects, so remediation is straightforward.

Performing Upgrade

With compatibility confirmed, we run the actual upgrade. PostgreSQL 18 offers traditional copy mode, **--link** which uses hard links, and the new **--swap** mode that exchanges directory contents between the two clusters. The **--swap** mode is potentially the fastest because it avoids both copying and linking, but it means the old cluster cannot be restarted if anything goes wrong.

For a production upgrade, we typically use **--link** to minimize downtime while keeping the old data files intact until we confirm the new cluster is healthy:

```
sudo -u postgres /usr/lib/postgresql/18/bin/pg_upgrade \
     --old-datadir=/var/lib/postgresql/16/main \
     --new-datadir=/var/lib/postgresql/18/main \
     --old-bindir=/usr/lib/postgresql/16/bin \
     --new-bindir=/usr/lib/postgresql/18/bin \
     --jobs=4 \
     --link
```

We omit **--no-statistics** so that **pg_upgrade** preserves optimizer statistics from the old cluster. This is the single most impactful PostgreSQL 18 improvement for production upgrades. In earlier versions the upgraded cluster started with no statistics at all, forcing the query planner to generate inefficient execution plans until a full **ANALYZE** finished. On large databases that **ANALYZE** could take hours, during which time production queries ran slowly or timed out.

With PostgreSQL 18, the new cluster starts with nearly complete statistics already in place, and the post-upgrade **ANALYZE** reduces to a quick fill-in of the few categories (such as extended statistics) that are not automatically preserved.

The following summary table compares the three file-handling modes available in PostgreSQL 18's **pg_upgrade**:

Mode	Speed	Cluster After Upgrade	Best For
copy	Slowest	Intact and restartable	Small databases or dev/test
--link	Fast	Intact but files shared; do not restart	Most production upgrades
--clone	Fast	Independent copy via reflink	XFS or Btrfs with CoW
--swap	Fastest	Not restartable; directories swapped	Planned cutovers where rollback is by snapshot

Post-Upgrade Steps and Verification

At this point, we will start the new PostgreSQL 18 cluster and run the lightweight post-upgrade statistics fill-in recommended by the **pg_upgrade** output. In the following commands, we will proceed:

```
# Start the new cluster:
sudo systemctl start postgresql@18-main

# Fill in any statistics that pg_upgrade could not transfer:
sudo -u postgres /usr/lib/postgresql/18/bin/vacuumdb \
     --all --analyze-in-stages --missing-stats-only --jobs=4

# Then trigger a full analyze pass for cumulative statistics:
sudo -u postgres /usr/lib/postgresql/18/bin/vacuumdb \
     --all --analyze-only --jobs=4
```

The **--missing-stats-only** option is new in PostgreSQL 18 and is designed specifically for this post-upgrade scenario. It populates statistics only for objects that do not already have them, which in practice means a handful of expression indexes and extended statistics objects that **pg_upgrade** cannot preserve automatically. The subsequent **--analyze-only** pass ensures cumulative statistics tracking is current so that autovacuum and autoanalyze can schedule correctly. Both commands run in parallel thanks to **--jobs=4**, mirroring the parallelism we used during the upgrade itself.

So, let us verify the upgrade by connecting to the new cluster and confirming the version, schema inventory, and row counts:

```
psql -U postgres -d cookbook_db

SELECT version();
\dn
SELECT n_tup_ins, n_tup_upd, n_tup_del
FROM   pg_stat_all_tables
WHERE  schemaname = 'hr' AND relname = 'employees';
```

The version string must show **PostgreSQL 18.0** or later, every schema from the old cluster must be present, and row counts must match the pre-upgrade baseline. Once verification passes and a period of production traffic has confirmed the new cluster is healthy, we remove the old cluster's files using the cleanup script that **pg_upgrade** generates in the working directory. Until that point, the old data remains available as a rollback option, assuming we used **--copy** or **--clone** rather than **--link** or **--swap**.

Summary

This chapter covered the full spectrum of database migration techniques available for PostgreSQL 18. We moved our **cookbook_db** sample application from an on-premises server to AWS EC2 and RDS using native **pg_dump** and **pg_restore** flows, orchestrated a managed migration using AWS Data Migration Service with near-zero downtime via change data capture, and consolidated data from EC2 to RDS using the **aws rds restore-db-instance-from-s3** command. Each of these patterns has distinct tradeoffs between operational complexity, downtime, and cost, giving us options to match the demands of any migration scenario.

We also addressed cross-engine migrations using **pgloader** to bring MySQL data into PostgreSQL with explicit type casts for **datetime**, **date**, and **tinyint** incompatibilities, and we set up a MySQL Foreign Data Wrapper that exposes remote MySQL tables directly inside PostgreSQL as foreign tables. The FDW approach is especially valuable for phased migrations where legacy applications must continue operating against the original MySQL backend while new applications query the consolidated PostgreSQL cluster.

Most significantly, this edition added a new recipe for upgrading existing PostgreSQL clusters to version 18 using **pg_upgrade**. We walked through the full upgrade flow including the checksum compatibility considerations introduced in Chapter 1, the new parallel **--jobs** option for compatibility checks, the **--swap** directory-exchange mode, and most importantly the automatic preservation of optimizer statistics across the major version boundary. We closed with the new **vacuumdb --missing-stats-only** post-upgrade command that completes the statistics coverage in seconds rather than hours.

CHAPTER 5
WAL, I/O, AUTOVACUUM AND ARCHIVELOG

Introduction

This chapter takes us deep into the internal maintenance and I/O subsystems that keep PostgreSQL healthy, performant, and recoverable under production workloads. We will start with Write-Ahead Logging (WAL), enabling compression to reduce WAL file sizes and configuring performance parameters that govern write throughput, checkpoint frequency, and replication lag. We will then set up continuous archiving and remote WAL archive destinations for point-in-time recovery and disaster preparedness.

From there, we will explore the vacuum process, covering the PostgreSQL 18 enhancements that include eager freezing of all-visible pages, the new **`vacuum_truncate`** server variable, and the behavioral change that causes **`VACUUM`** and **`ANALYZE`** to recurse into inheritance children by default. We will debug and optimize autovacuum using the new timing columns added to **`pg_stat_all_tables`** in this release, including **`total_vacuum_time`**, **`total_autovacuum_time`**, and **`total_analyze_time`**. Finally, we will put the asynchronous I/O (AIO) subsystem feature into practice, which allows the server to queue multiple read requests simultaneously, overlapping disk fetches with query processing for dramatically improved throughput on sequential scans, bitmap heap scans, and vacuum operations.

Every recipe in this chapter operates against the **`cookbook_db`** database and the schemas we built across Chapters 1 through 4. We will generate workload against our **`hr.employees`**, **`sales.orders`**, and **`production.products`** tables to observe WAL generation, vacuum behavior, and I/O patterns in real time.

Recipe #1: Enabling WAL Compression

Write-Ahead Logging records every data modification before it reaches the actual data files, providing crash recovery and replication support. Each WAL record consumes disk space, and on a busy database the WAL directory can grow rapidly, consuming storage and increasing the I/O cost of archiving and shipping. The activation of WAL compression reduces the size of the data portion of WAL records using a lightweight algorithm, which shrinks WAL file sizes and lowers the bandwidth required for replication and archiving.

In this recipe, we enable compression and observe its impact on our **`cookbook_db`** workload.

Enable WAL Compression

We now proceed to open the PostgreSQL configuration file. As we configured the installation path in Chapter 1, the file resides at **`/etc/postgresql/18/main/postgresql.conf`** for binary installations. At this stage, we will then run the following command:

```
sudo nano /etc/postgresql/18/main/postgresql.conf
```

We locate the **wal_compression** parameter and set it to **on**. In PostgreSQL 18, this parameter also accepts the values **pglz**, **lz4**, and **zstd** to select a specific algorithm. The **lz4** method offers the best balance of speed and compression ratio for most workloads, while **zstd** achieves higher compression at the cost of slightly more CPU time. Here, we will set the parameter as follows:

```
wal_compression = lz4
```

We restart the PostgreSQL service to apply the change:

```
sudo systemctl restart postgresql
```

Observe Impact

So here, we will then verify that the parameter is active and then generate a write workload against our **cookbook_db** tables to observe the effect on WAL file sizes. We will then connect to the database and run the following SQL to confirm the setting and to generate WAL activity:

```
SHOW wal_compression;


-- Generate write workload against our sample tables:
INSERT INTO sales.orders (customer_name, employee_id, order_date,
total_due, territory)
SELECT
    'BulkCustomer-' || g,
    (g % 3) + 1,
    CURRENT_DATE - (g % 90),
    round((random() * 5000 + 100)::numeric, 2),
    CASE g % 4
        WHEN 0 THEN 'South Asia'
        WHEN 1 THEN 'Europe'
        WHEN 2 THEN 'North America'
        ELSE 'Asia Pacific'
    END
```

```
FROM generate_series(1, 10000) AS g;
```

After the insert completes, we check the WAL directory to observe the file sizes:

```
sudo ls -lh /var/lib/postgresql/18/main/pg_wal/ | head -10
```

With compression enabled, the WAL segment files remain at 16 MB each (the default segment size), but fewer segments are generated for the same volume of data modifications compared to an uncompressed configuration. The compression happens at the record level inside each segment, so the savings become visible as reduced segment turnover and lower archive bandwidth. We can also tune the complementary parameters **`wal_buffers`** and **`checkpoint_timeout`** to further optimize WAL performance, which we will cover in Recipe #2.

Recipe #2: Configuring WAL Performance Parameters

Beyond compression, PostgreSQL provides a rich set of parameters that control WAL write throughput, checkpoint behavior, and the trade-off between performance and recovery time. In this recipe, we configure the primary WAL performance parameters for our **`cookbook_db`** instance, monitor the results using built-in system views, and fine-tune the settings based on observed workload characteristics.

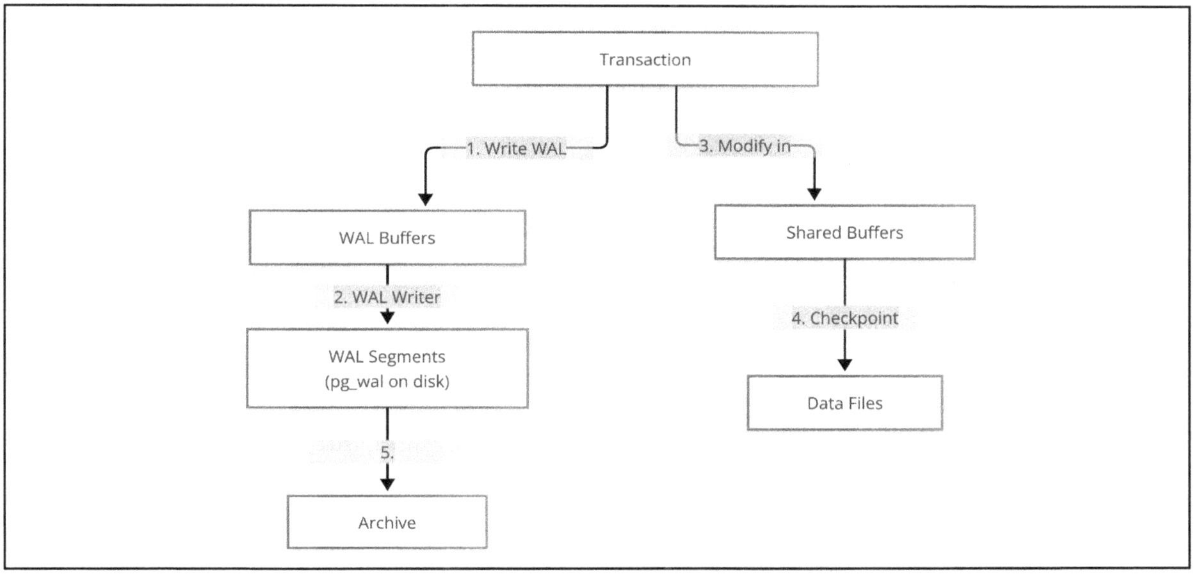

Fig 5.1: WAL Architecture and Checkpoint Cycle

Adjust WAL Performance Parameters

We will now open **postgresql.conf** and configure the following parameters. Each one controls a different aspect of the WAL and checkpoint pipeline. At this point, we will add or modify the following settings:

```
# WAL level: 'replica' supports physical replication and PITR;
# 'logical' is required for logical replication (Chapter 7).
wal_level = replica

# WAL buffer size: larger values reduce fsync frequency during
bursts.
wal_buffers = 64MB

# Checkpoint frequency: longer intervals reduce I/O overhead but
# increase recovery time after a crash.
checkpoint_timeout = 15min

# Maximum WAL between checkpoints: controls how much WAL
accumulates
# before a time-based or size-based checkpoint triggers.
max_wal_size = 4GB
min_wal_size = 256MB

# Synchronous commit: 'on' ensures durability; 'off' improves
# write throughput but risks losing the most recent transactions
# after a crash. We keep it on for production safety.
synchronous_commit = on
```

We restart the service to apply the changes. In the following command, we will:

```
sudo systemctl restart postgresql
```

Monitor WAL Performance

So, let us use PostgreSQL's built-in views to confirm our settings are active and to observe checkpoint and archiving activity. With this in mind, we will now connect to **cookbook_db** and run the following SQL queries:

```
-- Checkpoint activity:
SELECT checkpoints_timed, checkpoints_req,
       buffers_checkpoint, buffers_clean, buffers_backend
FROM pg_stat_bgwriter;

-- Archiver status:
SELECT archived_count, last_archived_wal, last_archived_time
FROM pg_stat_archiver;

-- Replication lag (if replicas are connected):
SELECT client_addr,
       pg_wal_lsn_diff(sent_lsn, replay_lsn) AS
replication_lag_bytes
FROM pg_stat_replication;
```

The **checkpoints_timed** value should be significantly higher than **checkpoints_req**. If **checkpoints_req** is growing rapidly, it means the WAL is hitting **max_wal_size** before **checkpoint_timeout** triggers, indicating that we should increase **max_wal_size** or reduce the write rate. A healthy ratio is at least 90 percent timed checkpoints to 10 percent requested checkpoints. We will revisit these metrics in Chapter 7 when we configure replication and monitor replica lag.

Recipe #3: Administering Continuous Archive

Continuous archiving copies every completed WAL segment to a durable archive location, enabling Point-in-Time Recovery (PITR) to any moment within the archive window. This capability is the foundation for both disaster recovery and the incremental backup strategies we will configure in Chapter 10. In this recipe, we enable continuous archiving on our **cookbook_db** server and verify that WAL segments flow to the designated archive directory.

Configure Archive Mode

We now proceed to open **postgresql.conf** and set the archive parameters. The **archive_mode** parameter enables archiving, and the **archive_command** parameter specifies the command that PostgreSQL executes to copy each completed WAL segment to the archive. At this stage, we will then add the following settings:

```
archive_mode = on
archive_command = 'cp %p /var/lib/postgresql/wal_archive/%f'
```

Here, we will create the archive directory and ensure the **postgres** user has write permissions:

```
sudo mkdir -p /var/lib/postgresql/wal_archive
sudo chown postgres:postgres /var/lib/postgresql/wal_archive
sudo systemctl restart postgresql
```

After the restart, we create a manual checkpoint and verify that WAL files appear in the archive directory. So here, we will then run the following SQL and shell command:

```
SELECT pg_switch_wal();
ls -lh /var/lib/postgresql/wal_archive/
```

The output should list at least one WAL segment file with a 24-character hexadecimal filename, confirming that the archive pipeline is operational. We then monitor the archiver status with the **pg_stat_archiver** view that we used in Recipe #2 to track **archived_count** and detect any archiving failures via **failed_count**. If **failed_count** is non-zero, the PostgreSQL log will contain the specific error from the **archive_command** execution, which is typically a permission or disk-space issue on the archive destination.

Manage Archive Retention

Archived WAL segments accumulate over time and will eventually exhaust the archive storage. We will then implement a retention policy using a cron job that removes segments older than 30 days:

```
sudo crontab -u postgres -e

# Add the following line to run daily at 2:00 AM:
0 2 * * * find /var/lib/postgresql/wal_archive -type f -mtime +30 -
delete
```

This cron job scans the archive directory every night at 2:00 AM and deletes any WAL files whose modification timestamp is more than 30 days old. We should adjust the retention period to match our recovery window requirements and backup strategy, which we will configure in detail in Chapter 10. For environments with more sophisticated retention needs, we can use tools such as **pgBackRest** that manage retention policies automatically and integrate with both local and S3 archive destinations.

Recipe #4: Using Remote WAL Archive Options

Local archiving protects against data file corruption but not against host-level failures such as disk loss or data center outages. Remote WAL archiving transfers completed WAL segments to a separate server or object store, providing geographic redundancy and supporting cross-site disaster recovery. In this recipe, we configure our **cookbook_db** server to archive WAL segments to a remote host using **rsync** over SSH with key-based authentication.

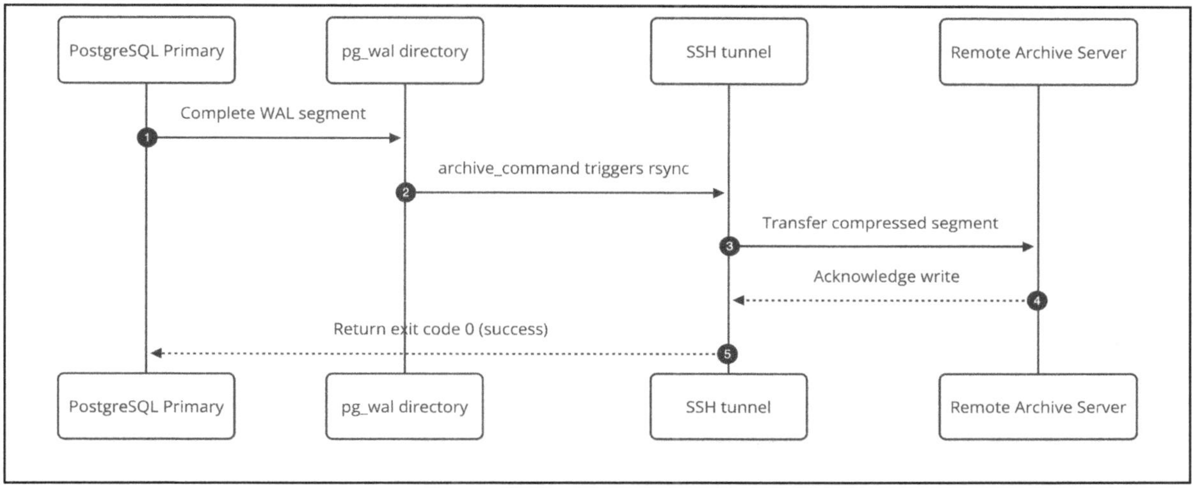

Fig 5.2: Remote WAL Archive Flow

Setup SSH Keys for Secure Transfer

We will now generate an SSH key pair for the **postgres** system user and copy the public key to the remote archive server. This setup enables passwordless transfers, which is necessary because **archive_command** runs as a non-interactive process that cannot prompt for credentials. At this point, we will run the following commands as the **postgres** user:

```
sudo -i -u postgres
ssh-keygen -t ed25519 -N '' -f ~/.ssh/id_ed25519
ssh-copy-id -i ~/.ssh/id_ed25519.pub archive_user@192.0.2.10
ssh archive_user@192.0.2.10 'echo Connection OK'
```

The final command tests the connection without a password prompt, confirming that key-based authentication works. We will now update **postgresql.conf** to use **rsync** with compression for the archive command. So here, we will add the following setting:

```
archive_command = 'rsync -az %p
archive_user@192.0.2.10:/mnt/wal_archive/%f'
```

The **-a** flag preserves file metadata, and the **-z** flag enables in-transit compression to reduce network bandwidth consumption. We restart the service and verify that segments arrive on the remote server by running **pg_switch_wal()** and then checking the remote archive directory via SSH. At this point, we monitor the **pg_stat_archiver** view to confirm that **archived_count** increments and **failed_count** remains at zero.

If archiving failures occur, common causes include SSH key permissions (the private key must be **600**), firewall rules blocking port **22** between the primary and the archive server, or insufficient disk space on the remote destination.

Verify and Monitor Remote Archive

We now verify that WAL segments are reaching the remote archive server by querying the pg_stat_archiver system view, which tracks every archive attempt made since the server started. At this stage, we run the following query on the primary server to inspect the current archiving health:

```
SELECT archived_count,
       last_archived_wal,
       last_archived_time,
       failed_count,
       last_failed_wal,
       last_failed_time
FROM pg_stat_archiver;
```

The archived_count field shows the total number of WAL segments successfully transferred to the remote host. We confirm that last_archived_wal is recent and that failed_count remains at zero. A non-zero failed_count tells us that our archive_command encountered an error during transfer, and we inspect last_failed_wal alongside the server log to diagnose the issue.

We also log in to the remote archive server and verify that WAL files are accumulating in the expected directory with the correct ownership and permissions for the archive_user account we configured in the first subsection of this recipe.

Recipe #5: Exploring Vacuum Process

The **VACUUM** process reclaims storage occupied by dead tuples left behind by **UPDATE** and **DELETE** operations, updates the visibility map for index-only scans, and prevents transaction ID wraparound.

In PostgreSQL 18, the vacuum subsystem receives three significant enhancements. They are freezing of all-visible pages to distribute anti-wraparound work across regular vacuum runs, a new server-level **vacuum_truncate** variable that controls whether vacuum truncates empty pages at the end of table files, and a behavioral change that makes **VACUUM** and **ANALYZE** automatically recurse into child tables of inheritance hierarchies (including declarative partitions) by default.

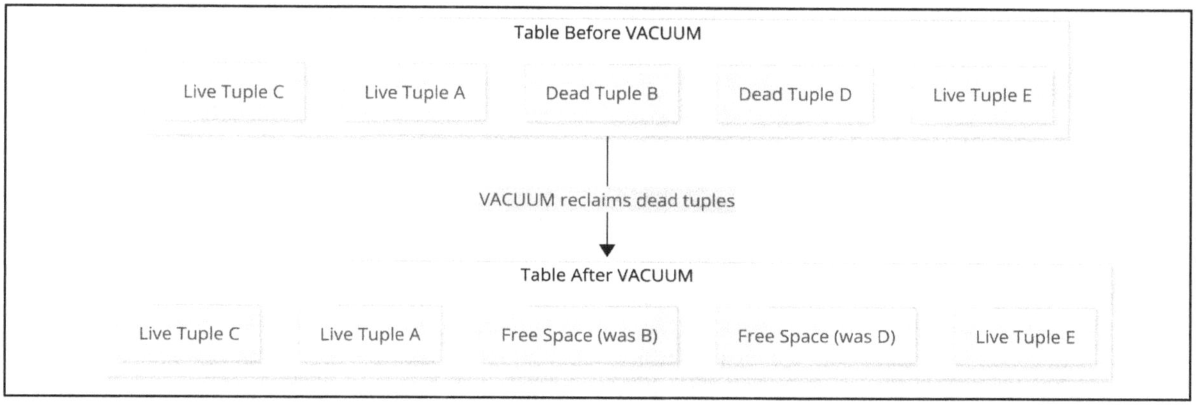

Fig 5.3: MVCC and Vacuum Dead Tuple Reclamation

Perform Standard and Full Vacuum Operations

So, let us connect to **cookbook_db** and generate dead tuples in our **sales.orders** table by performing a batch update followed by a standard **VACUUM** operation.

```
-- Generate dead tuples by updating rows in bulk:
UPDATE sales.orders SET total_due = total_due * 1.05
WHERE territory = 'Europe';

-- Check dead tuple accumulation before vacuuming:
SELECT relname, n_live_tup, n_dead_tup
FROM pg_stat_user_tables
WHERE schemaname = 'sales' AND relname = 'orders';

-- Perform standard VACUUM on the table:
VACUUM VERBOSE sales.orders;
```

The **VERBOSE** flag produces detailed output showing how many dead tuples were removed, how many pages were scanned, and how many pages were truncated from the end of the file. After the vacuum completes, we re-query **pg_stat_user_tables** to confirm that **n_dead_tup** has dropped to zero or near-zero for the **sales.orders** table. For situations where the table has accumulated significant bloat over time, we can run **VACUUM FULL** which rewrites the entire table into a new file, reclaiming all wasted space.

However, **VACUUM FULL** acquires an exclusive lock on the table, so it should only be used during maintenance windows. Hence, we proceed to run the following:

```
VACUUM FULL VERBOSE sales.orders;
```

Vacuum Enhancements

The first major enhancement in PostgreSQL 18 is eager freezing of all-visible pages during regular vacuum runs. Previously, freezing tuples to prevent transaction ID wraparound was performed only during an aggressive anti-wraparound vacuum pass, which could be disruptive and time-consuming on large tables. In PostgreSQL 18, the regular vacuum process opportunistically freezes tuples on all-visible pages as it encounters them, distributing the freezing workload across many smaller runs rather than concentrating it in a single large pass.

The new **vacuum_max_eager_freeze_failure_rate** parameter controls how aggressive this behavior is, with a default of **0.03** (3 percent), meaning the vacuum process will tolerate up to 3 percent of pages failing the eager freeze check before falling back to the traditional approach.

We can query the current setting as below:

```
SHOW vacuum_max_eager_freeze_failure_rate;
```

The second enhancement is the new **vacuum_truncate** server variable. In prior versions, truncation behavior (removing empty pages from the physical end of a table file to shrink it on disk) could only be controlled per-table via a storage parameter. PostgreSQL 18 adds a server-wide default that we can set in **postgresql.conf**. On systems with hot standby replicas that serve read traffic, setting **vacuum_truncate = off** prevents access-exclusive locks during truncation that could cause query cancellations on the replica.

Here, we will run the following to configure this for a specific table:

```
-- Server-wide default (in postgresql.conf):
-- vacuum_truncate = off


-- Override for a specific table during maintenance windows:
```

```
ALTER TABLE sales.orders SET (vacuum_truncate = on);
VACUUM VERBOSE sales.orders;
ALTER TABLE sales.orders RESET (vacuum_truncate);
```

The third enhancement changes how **VACUUM** and **ANALYZE** handle inheritance hierarchies. In PostgreSQL 18, these commands automatically process all child tables (including declarative partitions) by default when run against a parent table. If we want to target only the parent without touching its children, we use the new **ONLY** keyword.

We demonstrate this with the partitioned **sales.orders** table, assuming we add partitions in Chapter 6 with the following query.

```
-- PostgreSQL 18 default: VACUUM processes parent AND all children
VACUUM ANALYZE sales.orders;

-- Target only the parent table, skip children:
VACUUM ANALYZE ONLY sales.orders;
```

Recipe #6: Debugging PostgreSQL Autovacuum

The autovacuum daemon automatically triggers **VACUUM** and **ANALYZE** operations based on table activity thresholds, preventing bloat and maintaining up-to-date optimizer statistics without manual intervention. When autovacuum is not keeping pace with write activity, tables accumulate dead tuples, query plans degrade, and eventually the system risks transaction ID wraparound. In this recipe, we debug and optimize autovacuum on our **cookbook_db** instance using both traditional techniques and the new PostgreSQL 18 observability features.

Check Autovacuum Settings and Activity

We begin by reviewing the current autovacuum configuration. So here, we will then connect to **cookbook_db** and run the following:

```
SELECT name, setting, short_desc
FROM pg_settings
WHERE name LIKE 'autovacuum%'
ORDER BY name;
```

The PostgreSQL 18 introduces an important operational change, which is reloadable **autovacuum_max_workers** without a server restart. Previously, changing the worker limit required a full restart, which was disruptive in production environments. The new approach separates the concept into two parameters. One is **autovacuum_worker_slots** that sets the maximum number of reserved slots at startup (still requires a restart), and the other is **autovacuum_max_workers** which controls how many of those slots are active concurrently (reloadable via **pg_reload_conf()**).

This separation allows us to reserve capacity upfront and then scale the active worker count up or down on the fly in response to workload changes. We identify tables that may be struggling with dead tuple accumulation by querying the statistics view as below:

```
SELECT schemaname, relname, n_dead_tup, n_live_tup,
       last_autovacuum, autovacuum_count
FROM pg_stat_user_tables
WHERE n_dead_tup > 1000
ORDER BY n_dead_tup DESC;
```

Maintenance Timing Columns

PostgreSQL 18 adds four new timing columns to the **pg_stat_all_tables** view that track cumulative time spent on maintenance operations. They are **total_vacuum_time** (time spent on manual vacuums), **total_autovacuum_time** (time spent on automatic vacuums), **total_analyze_time** (time spent on manual analyzes), and **total_autoanalyze_time** (time spent on automatic analyzes). These columns make it straightforward to identify which tables consume the most maintenance resources.

So in the below, we will now run to find our top maintenance consumers:

```
SELECT relname,
       total_vacuum_time,
       total_autovacuum_time,
       total_analyze_time,
       total_autoanalyze_time,
       vacuum_count,
       autovacuum_count,
       pg_size_pretty(pg_total_relation_size(
           schemaname || '.' || relname)) AS table_size
FROM pg_stat_all_tables
WHERE schemaname NOT IN ('pg_catalog', 'information_schema')
```

```
ORDER BY (COALESCE(total_vacuum_time, 0) +
          COALESCE(total_autovacuum_time, 0)) DESC
LIMIT 10;
```

If a table shows high **total_autovacuum_time** relative to its size and activity, it may benefit from more frequent but lighter vacuums, which we achieve by lowering its **autovacuum_vacuum_scale_factor** or setting the new **autovacuum_vacuum_max_threshold** (also new in PostgreSQL 18) to cap the dead tuple accumulation before triggering. We also enable the **track_cost_delay_timing** parameter to measure how much time vacuum operations spend sleeping due to cost-based delays.

So here, following is the quick SQL query:

```
ALTER SYSTEM SET track_cost_delay_timing = on;
SELECT pg_reload_conf();
```

With this enabled, the **pg_stat_progress_vacuum** view includes a **delay_time** column showing cumulative delay. If a vacuum run shows a delay time that dominates its total duration, it means cost-based throttling is the bottleneck, and we should increase **vacuum_cost_limit** or reduce **vacuum_cost_delay** for that table. Conversely, if the delay time is near zero but the vacuum still takes a long time, the bottleneck is disk I/O, and the new asynchronous I/O subsystem in Recipe #7 becomes the relevant optimization lever.

Tune Autovacuum for High-Churn Tables

For tables in our **cookbook_db** that receive frequent writes, such as **sales.orders**, we apply table-specific autovacuum settings that trigger vacuums earlier and allow them to run faster.

```
ALTER TABLE sales.orders SET (
    autovacuum_vacuum_scale_factor = 0.02,
    autovacuum_analyze_scale_factor = 0.01,
    autovacuum_vacuum_cost_delay = 0
);

-- For very large tables, cap the dead tuple threshold:
ALTER TABLE sales.orders SET (
    autovacuum_vacuum_max_threshold = 50000
);
```

The **autovacuum_vacuum_max_threshold** is new in PostgreSQL 18 and sets a hard upper limit on the number of dead tuples that can accumulate before autovacuum triggers, regardless of the percentage-based scale factor. For large tables with millions of rows, the default scale factor of **0.2** could allow millions of dead tuples before cleanup begins. The hard cap prevents that runaway accumulation while preserving the percentage-based formula for smaller tables, giving us the best of both approaches.

Recipe #7: Leveraging Asynchronous I/O Subsystem

PostgreSQL 18 introduces a fundamentally new approach to how the server reads data from disk. The asynchronous I/O (AIO) subsystem allows backend and maintenance processes to queue multiple read requests simultaneously rather than waiting for each one to complete before issuing the next. This overlapping of I/O operations with CPU work dramatically reduces the wall-clock time for operations that are dominated by disk reads, including sequential scans on large tables, bitmap heap scans, and the heap scan phase of **VACUUM**.

In this recipe, we configure the AIO subsystem, observe its behavior through the new **pg_aios** system view, and benchmark its impact on our **cookbook_db** workload.

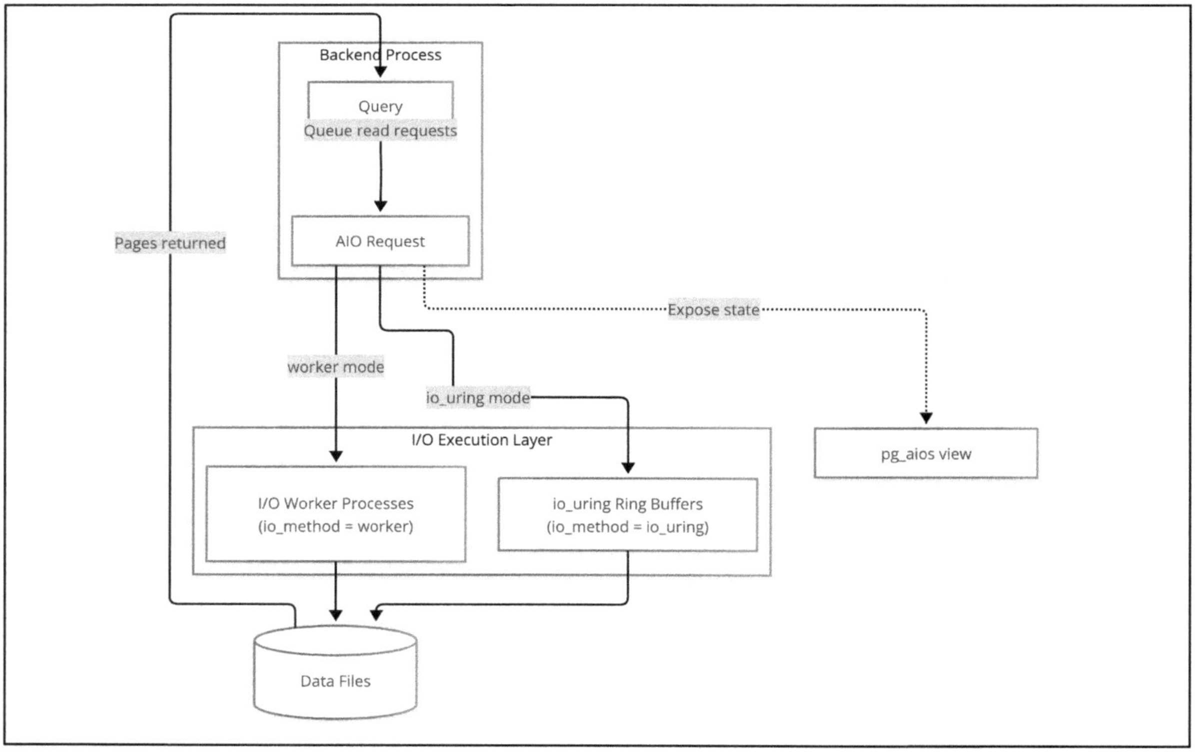

Fig 5.4: Asynchronous I/O Subsystem Architecture

Configure I/O Method

As we introduced in Chapter 1 Recipe #6, the **io_method** parameter controls which strategy PostgreSQL uses for asynchronous reads. The three options are **worker** (the default, which delegates reads to background I/O worker processes), **io_uring** (which uses the Linux kernel's **io_uring** interface for zero-copy reads, requiring compilation with **--with-liburing** as we did in Chapter 1 Recipe #3), and **sync** (which preserves the traditional blocking read behavior from PostgreSQL 17). In the following script, we will verify our current setting and related parameters.

So, let us connect again to **cookbook_db** and run the following:

```
SELECT name, setting, short_desc
FROM pg_settings
WHERE name IN (
    'io_method',
    'io_workers',
    'effective_io_concurrency',
    'maintenance_io_concurrency',
    'io_combine_limit',
    'io_max_combine_limit'
)
ORDER BY name;
```

The terminal will display below output:

```
          name          | setting |                    short_desc
------------------------+---------+---------------------------------------
------------
 effective_io_concurrency | 16    | Number of concurrent disk I/O
operations
 io_combine_limit       | 128     | Limit on combining I/O requests
 io_max_combine_limit   | 128     | Maximum limit on combining I/O
requests
 io_method              | worker  | Method used for asynchronous I/O
 io_workers             | 3       | Number of I/O worker processes
 maintenance_io_concurrency | 16  | Concurrent I/O for maintenance
```

```
work
```

The **io_workers** parameter sets the number of background I/O worker processes (default **3**). Each worker can service one I/O request at a time, so increasing this value allows more concurrent disk reads. The **io_combine_limit** parameter controls how many pages can be combined into a single I/O operation, allowing the kernel to issue larger reads that are more efficient on modern storage hardware. Both **effective_io_concurrency** and **maintenance_io_concurrency** have been raised from their previous default of **1** to **16** in PostgreSQL 18, reflecting the capabilities of SSDs and cloud block storage.

Monitor AIO Activity with 'pg_aios'

PostgreSQL 18 provides a new system view called **pg_aios** that exposes the state of active asynchronous I/O operations. This view shows which file handles have pending I/O requests, enabling us to observe AIO behavior in real time during sequential scans, bitmap heap scans, and vacuum operations. With this in mind, we will now run a sequential scan on a large table in one session and observe **pg_aios** from a second session.

In the first session we run the following:

```
-- Session 1: Trigger a sequential scan on a large table
EXPLAIN (ANALYZE, BUFFERS) SELECT * FROM sales.orders
WHERE total_due > 1000;
```

In a second session, while the scan is in progress, we query the **pg_aios** view as below:

```
-- Session 2: Observe active AIO operations
SELECT * FROM pg_aios;
```

The output shows active file descriptors, the operation type (read), and the status of each pending request. Under the **worker** I/O method, we will see entries corresponding to the I/O worker processes that are fetching pages ahead of the query executor. Under the **io_uring** method, the entries correspond to kernel-level ring buffer submissions. If the view is empty, the scan completed before we could observe it; we can use larger tables or add a **pg_sleep** pause in the scan to extend the observation window.

Tune AIO for Production Workloads

For our **cookbook_db** environment running on SSD-backed storage, we increase the I/O worker pool and concurrency settings to take full advantage of the hardware. At this stage, we will then add the following settings to **postgresql.conf**:

```
# Increase I/O worker pool for higher concurrency:
```

```
io_workers = 6

# Raise concurrency for query and maintenance operations:
effective_io_concurrency = 32
maintenance_io_concurrency = 32

# Allow larger combined I/O requests (256 pages per request):
io_combine_limit = 256
```

We restart the service and repeat the sequential scan benchmark. The **EXPLAIN (ANALYZE, BUFFERS)** output will show reduced execution time for the scan because the server now pre-fetches pages asynchronously while the executor processes previously fetched pages. The improvement is most dramatic for cold-cache workloads (when data is not in shared buffers) and for large sequential scans and vacuum operations that would otherwise stall on individual synchronous reads.

On NVMe storage, the **io_uring** method can reduce I/O latency even further by eliminating the overhead of worker process context switching, but it requires kernel 5.1 or later and the **--with-liburing** compile flag that we used in Chapter 1.

The following table summarizes the recommended AIO tuning ranges based on storage type:

Parameter	HDD	SSD (SATA/SAS)	NVMe
io_method	worker	worker or io_uring	io_uring preferred
io_workers	3 (default)	6 to 8	3
effective_io_concurrency	4	32	64 to 200
maintenance_io_concurrency	4	32	64 to 200
io_combine_limit	128 (default)	256	256

We should increase these values gradually and monitor disk utilization using system tools such as **iostat** and **iotop** alongside the PostgreSQL **pg_aios** and **pg_stat_io** views. Over-provisioning concurrency beyond the hardware's capability results in I/O queue saturation and increased latency, which degrades rather than improves performance. The goal is to keep the storage device busy without overwhelming it, and the observability tools in PostgreSQL 18 give us the visibility to find that balance.

We will revisit AIO performance in context when we configure vacuum on partitioned tables in Chapter 6 and during replication workloads in Chapter 7.

Summary

This chapter covered the internal maintenance and I/O subsystems that keep our

cookbook_db database healthy and performant under production workloads. We enabled WAL compression using the **lz4** algorithm to reduce segment sizes and archive bandwidth, then configured the core WAL performance parameters governing checkpoint frequency, buffer sizes, and synchronous commit behavior.

Next, we set up continuous archiving to a local directory and extended it to a remote server with SSH key-based **rsync** transfers, establishing the foundation for the disaster recovery and backup strategies we will build upon in Chapters 10 and 11. We explored the vacuum process in depth, taking advantage of PostgreSQL 18 enhancements. And finally, we put the headline I/O feature of PostgreSQL 18 into practice by configuring the asynchronous I/O subsystem. We explored the **io_method** options (**worker**, **io_uring**, and **sync**), monitored live AIO activity through the new **pg_aios** view, and tuned **io_workers**, **effective_io_concurrency**, and **io_combine_limit** for SSD and NVMe storage.

CHAPTER 6
PARTITIONING AND SHARDING STRATEGIES

Introduction

This chapter takes us through the partitioning and sharding strategies that allow PostgreSQL to manage datasets far larger than any single table or server can handle efficiently. We will start by setting up range, list, and hash partitioning on our **cookbook_db** tables, taking advantage of the improved partition query planning and wider partitionwise join support introduced in PostgreSQL 18.

We will then explore vertical and horizontal partitioning patterns, learn how to dynamically attach, detach, and drop partitions for lifecycle management, and implement the older table-inheritance approach for scenarios where declarative partitioning does not provide sufficient flexibility.

We will automate partition creation with a PL/pgSQL function and **pg_cron**, run declarative partitioning with the PostgreSQL 18 enhancement that relaxes the unique index requirement to include non-btree index types, and finally configure sharding with Foreign Data Wrappers and Citus to distribute our database across multiple nodes.

Recipe #1: Setting up Partitioning

The partitioning divides a single large table into smaller physical segments called partitions, each holding a subset of the rows.

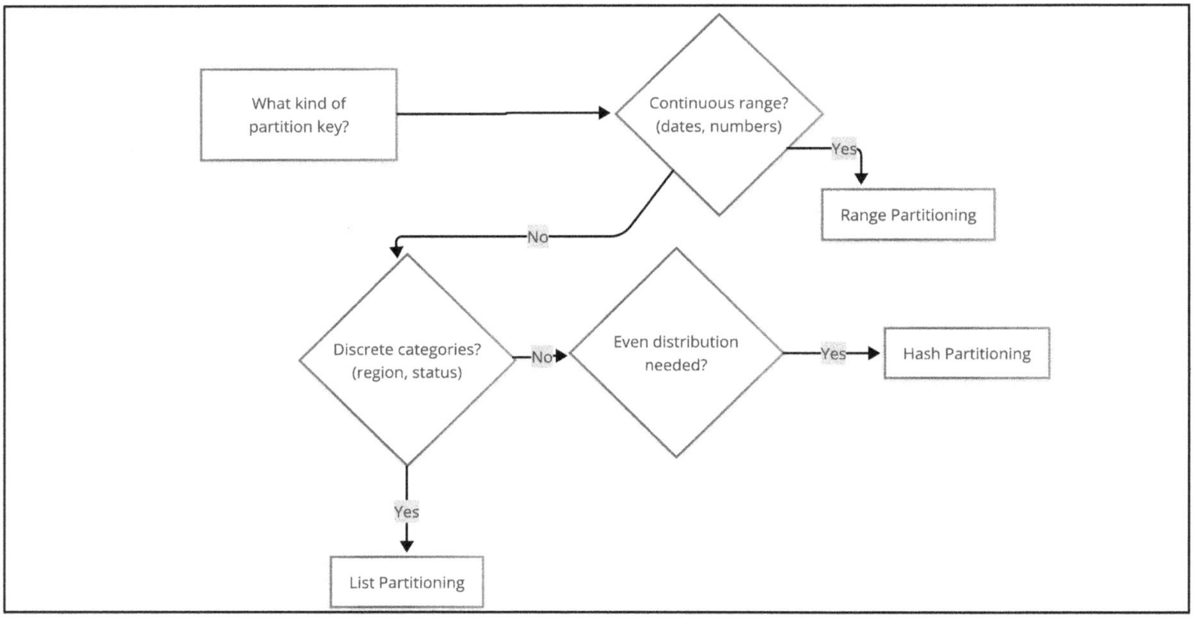

Fig 6.1: Partition Strategy Decision Tree

The PostgreSQL routes queries and inserts to the correct partition automatically, and the query planner prunes partitions that cannot contain matching rows, dramatically reducing the amount of data scanned. The PostgreSQL supports range partitioning (continuous values such as dates or numeric ranges), list partitioning (discrete values such as territory codes or categories), and hash partitioning (even distribution based on a hash of the partition key) strategies.

In this recipe, we partition our **sales.orders** table by **order_date** using range partitioning and observe how PostgreSQL 18's improved partition query planning affects execution.

Define and Create Partitions

We will replace the non-partitioned **sales.orders** table with a partitioned equivalent. Because we already have data in the table from previous chapters, we rename the existing table, create the partitioned replacement, copy the data over, and then drop the original.

Here, we will connect to **cookbook_db** and run the following SQL:

```
-- Rename the existing table to preserve data:
ALTER TABLE sales.orders RENAME TO orders_legacy;


-- Create the partitioned table with the same structure:
CREATE TABLE sales.orders (
    order_id SERIAL,
    customer_name VARCHAR(100) NOT NULL,
    employee_id INT REFERENCES hr.employees(employee_id),
    order_date DATE DEFAULT CURRENT_DATE,
    total_due NUMERIC(12, 2),
    territory VARCHAR(50),
    PRIMARY KEY (order_id, order_date)
) PARTITION BY RANGE (order_date);


-- Create yearly partitions:
CREATE TABLE sales.orders_2024 PARTITION OF sales.orders
    FOR VALUES FROM ('2024-01-01') TO ('2025-01-01');


CREATE TABLE sales.orders_2025 PARTITION OF sales.orders
    FOR VALUES FROM ('2025-01-01') TO ('2026-01-01');
```

```
CREATE TABLE sales.orders_2026 PARTITION OF sales.orders
    FOR VALUES FROM ('2026-01-01') TO ('2027-01-01');

-- Copy existing data into the partitioned table:
INSERT INTO sales.orders (customer_name, employee_id,
    order_date, total_due, territory)
SELECT customer_name, employee_id,
    order_date, total_due, territory
FROM sales.orders_legacy;

-- Drop the legacy table:
DROP TABLE sales.orders_legacy;
```

The **`PRIMARY KEY (order_id, order_date)`** definition includes the partition key **`order_date`** alongside **`order_id`**. This is a PostgreSQL requirement. The unique and primary key constraints on partitioned tables must include all columns of the partition key so that each partition can enforce uniqueness locally without cross-partition coordination. The PostgreSQL automatically creates a matching primary key index on each partition child table.

Observe Partition Pruning and Partitionwise Joins

PostgreSQL 18 improves the query planner's ability to prune irrelevant partitions and to push join operations down to individual partitions (partitionwise joins). We can now verify that pruning is active by running an **`EXPLAIN`** on a date-filtered query.

```
EXPLAIN (ANALYZE, COSTS OFF)
SELECT order_id, customer_name, total_due
FROM sales.orders
WHERE order_date BETWEEN '2025-07-01' AND '2025-07-31';
```

The execution plan shows that the planner scans only the **`sales.orders_2025`** partition, completely skipping **`sales.orders_2024`** and **`sales.orders_2026`**. The terminal will display output similar to the following:

```
Append (actual time=0.015..0.042 rows=5 loops=1)
  ->  Seq Scan on orders_2025 orders_1 (actual time=0.012..0.035
```

```
rows=5 loops=1)
        Filter: ((order_date >= '2025-07-01') AND (order_date <=
'2025-07-31'))
Planning Time: 0.218 ms
Execution Time: 0.064 ms
```

We also enable partitionwise joins to allow the planner to push join conditions into individual partitions. We will then run the following SQL to demonstrate this with a join against the **hr.employees** table:

```
SET enable_partitionwise_join = on;


EXPLAIN (ANALYZE, COSTS OFF)
SELECT o.order_id, o.customer_name, e.full_name, o.total_due
FROM sales.orders o
JOIN hr.employees e ON e.employee_id = o.employee_id
WHERE o.order_date BETWEEN '2025-01-01' AND '2025-12-31';
```

With **enable_partitionwise_join** enabled, the planner performs the join inside the pruned partition rather than scanning all partitions first and then joining. This optimization reduces both memory consumption and execution time, and PostgreSQL 18 extends its applicability to more join patterns than previous versions, including cases where the join condition involves expressions rather than simple column references.

Recipe #2: Implementing Vertical and Horizontal Partitioning

Beyond the standard range, list, and hash strategies, the PostgreSQL supports vertical partitioning (splitting columns across tables) and horizontal partitioning (splitting rows across tables) pattern. Vertical partitioning is especially useful when a table contains large, infrequently accessed columns such as **TEXT**, **BYTEA**, or **JSONB** fields that inflate row size and reduce the number of rows that fit in shared buffers. Horizontal partitioning uses the same row-splitting techniques as declarative or inheritance-based partitioning, and is typically used when we want to distribute data across separate physical tablespaces or servers.

Implement Vertical Partitioning

We will now apply vertical partitioning to the **production.products** table we created in

Chapter 2. The **description** column contains large TOAST-eligible values that are rarely needed in listing queries, so we split it into a separate detail table with the following:

```
-- Create the detail table for large, infrequently accessed
columns:
CREATE TABLE production.product_details (
    product_id INT PRIMARY KEY
        REFERENCES production.products(product_id),
    description TEXT,
    specifications JSONB
);

-- Move existing description data to the detail table:
INSERT INTO production.product_details (product_id, description)
SELECT product_id, description
FROM production.products
WHERE description IS NOT NULL;

-- Drop the description column from the main table:
ALTER TABLE production.products DROP COLUMN description;
```

After this split, queries that list products with only their name, category, and price scan a much narrower row, fitting more rows per shared buffer page and improving cache hit ratios. When we need the full detail, we use a simple **JOIN** between **production.products** and **production.product_details**.

In the following SQL block, we will to verify:

```
SELECT p.product_id, p.product_name, p.list_price,
       pd.description
FROM production.products p
LEFT JOIN production.product_details pd
    ON p.product_id = pd.product_id
WHERE p.category = 'Bikes';
```

Implement Horizontal Partitioning

Horizontal partitioning distributes rows across separate tables based on a row-level criterion, exactly like declarative partitioning but sometimes implemented using the older inheritance model for backward compatibility or when custom routing logic is required. For our **cookbook_db**, the declarative approach in Recipe #1 already implements horizontal partitioning on the **sales.orders** table. If we need to partition by a discrete attribute like territory rather than a range, we use list partitioning instead.

So, let us create a list-partitioned inventory table:

```
CREATE TABLE production.inventory (
    inventory_id SERIAL,
    product_id INT NOT NULL,
    warehouse VARCHAR(50) NOT NULL,
    quantity INT DEFAULT 0,
    last_restocked DATE DEFAULT CURRENT_DATE,
    PRIMARY KEY (inventory_id, warehouse)
) PARTITION BY LIST (warehouse);

CREATE TABLE production.inventory_mumbai
    PARTITION OF production.inventory
    FOR VALUES IN ('Mumbai');

CREATE TABLE production.inventory_pune
    PARTITION OF production.inventory
    FOR VALUES IN ('Pune');

CREATE TABLE production.inventory_delhi
    PARTITION OF production.inventory
    FOR VALUES IN ('Delhi');

-- Seed data:
INSERT INTO production.inventory (product_id, warehouse, quantity)
SELECT p.product_id,
```

```
    CASE (p.product_id % 3)
        WHEN 0 THEN 'Mumbai'
        WHEN 1 THEN 'Pune'
        ELSE 'Delhi'
    END,
    (random() * 500 + 10)::int
FROM production.products p;
```

Each warehouse has its own physical partition, allowing us to detach and archive regional data independently, apply per-partition indexes, and take advantage of list-based partition pruning in queries that filter by **`warehouse`**. We will use this inventory table in Recipe #3 to demonstrate partition lifecycle management, and we will reference it again when we configure sharding in Recipe #7.

Recipe #3: Performing Attach, Detach, and Partition Drop

Production databases evolve over time, and partitions must be added for new data ranges, detached for archival, and dropped when data reaches the end of its retention window. PostgreSQL supports these lifecycle operations as lightweight DDL commands that do not require rewriting the parent table. In this recipe, we walk through all three operations on our **`sales.orders`** partitioned table.

Attach New Partition

We need a partition for 2027 as our application approaches the boundary of existing coverage. We now proceed to create a standalone table with the correct structure, optionally pre-populate it with migrated data, and then attach it to the partitioned parent:

```
-- Create the standalone table:
CREATE TABLE sales.orders_2027 (
    order_id SERIAL,
    customer_name VARCHAR(100) NOT NULL,
    employee_id INT,
    order_date DATE NOT NULL,
    total_due NUMERIC(12, 2),
    territory VARCHAR(50),
    PRIMARY KEY (order_id, order_date)
```

```
);

-- Attach it to the partitioned parent:
ALTER TABLE sales.orders
    ATTACH PARTITION sales.orders_2027
    FOR VALUES FROM ('2027-01-01') TO ('2028-01-01');
```

When we attach a partition, PostgreSQL scans the new table to verify that all existing rows fall within the declared range boundary. For large pre-populated tables, we can add a **CHECK** constraint matching the partition boundary before attaching, which allows PostgreSQL to skip the validation scan entirely. This optimization is especially valuable during data migrations where millions of rows are loaded before the table is attached to the parent.

Detach and Drop Partition

We detach the 2024 partition to archive it, converting it back into a standalone table that retains all its data but no longer participates in queries against **sales.orders**.

```
-- Detach the 2024 partition:
ALTER TABLE sales.orders
    DETACH PARTITION sales.orders_2024;

-- The detached table is now independent; we can query it directly:
SELECT count(*) FROM sales.orders_2024;

-- If the data is no longer needed, drop the table:
DROP TABLE sales.orders_2024;
```

The detaching is a metadata-only operation and completes almost instantly regardless of table size, making it ideal for scheduled archival workflows. PostgreSQL 18 also supports **DETACH PARTITION ... CONCURRENTLY**, which avoids holding an **ACCESS EXCLUSIVE** lock on the parent table during the detach, allowing concurrent reads and writes to continue against other partitions while the detach is processed. We can now verify the partition structure after our changes by querying the system catalog as shown below:

```
SELECT inhrelid::regclass AS partition_name,
       pg_get_expr(c.relpartbound, c.oid) AS partition_bound
```

```
FROM pg_inherits i
JOIN pg_class c ON c.oid = i.inhrelid
WHERE i.inhparent = 'sales.orders'::regclass
ORDER BY partition_name;
```

The output lists only the remaining partitions (2025, 2026, and the newly attached 2027), confirming that 2024 has been fully removed from the partition hierarchy. We will use this same catalog query in Recipe #5 to verify automatically created partitions.

Recipe #4: Partitioning Tables using Table Inheritance

Before declarative partitioning arrived in PostgreSQL 10, inheritance-based partitioning was the standard approach. It remains useful in scenarios requiring custom constraints, per-partition defaults, or additional columns on child tables that the declarative model does not support. In this recipe, we create an inheritance-based partitioned structure for a new **hr.attendance** table and highlight the PostgreSQL 18 behavioral change for **VACUUM** and **ANALYZE** on inheritance hierarchies.

Create Parent and Child Tables

We will then define a parent table and two child tables that inherit its structure, each with a **CHECK** constraint that defines the partition boundary:

```
-- Parent table:
CREATE TABLE hr.attendance (
    attendance_id SERIAL PRIMARY KEY,
    employee_id INT REFERENCES hr.employees(employee_id),
    attendance_date DATE NOT NULL,
    check_in TIME,
    check_out TIME
);

-- Child table for Q1 2026:
CREATE TABLE hr.attendance_2026q1 (
    CHECK (attendance_date >= '2026-01-01'
       AND attendance_date <  '2026-04-01')
```

```
) INHERITS (hr.attendance);

-- Child table for Q2 2026:
CREATE TABLE hr.attendance_2026q2 (
    CHECK (attendance_date >= '2026-04-01'
       AND attendance_date <  '2026-07-01')
) INHERITS (hr.attendance);

-- Create indexes on each child:
CREATE INDEX idx_att_2026q1_emp
    ON hr.attendance_2026q1 (employee_id);
CREATE INDEX idx_att_2026q2_emp
    ON hr.attendance_2026q2 (employee_id);
```

Unlike declarative partitioning, inheritance does not automatically route inserts to the correct child table. We need a trigger or rule to handle routing.

So here, we will now create a trigger function that inspects the **attendance_date** value and inserts the row into the appropriate child:

```
CREATE OR REPLACE FUNCTION hr.route_attendance()
RETURNS TRIGGER AS $$
BEGIN
    IF NEW.attendance_date >= '2026-01-01'
       AND NEW.attendance_date < '2026-04-01' THEN
        INSERT INTO hr.attendance_2026q1 VALUES (NEW.*);
    ELSIF NEW.attendance_date >= '2026-04-01'
       AND NEW.attendance_date < '2026-07-01' THEN
        INSERT INTO hr.attendance_2026q2 VALUES (NEW.*);
    ELSE
        RAISE EXCEPTION 'No partition for date %',
                        NEW.attendance_date;
    END IF;
    RETURN NULL;
```

```
END;
$$ LANGUAGE plpgsql;

CREATE TRIGGER trg_route_attendance
    BEFORE INSERT ON hr.attendance
    FOR EACH ROW
    EXECUTE FUNCTION hr.route_attendance();
```

PostgreSQL 18 VACUUM/ANALYZE Behavior on Inheritance

As we covered in Chapter 5 Recipe #5, PostgreSQL 18 changes the default behavior so that **VACUUM** and **ANALYZE** automatically recurse into all child tables of an inheritance hierarchy. In previous versions, running **VACUUM ANALYZE hr.attendance** would only process the parent table itself, leaving the child tables untouched unless explicitly named. In PostgreSQL 18, the same command processes **hr.attendance**, **hr.attendance_2026q1**, and **hr.attendance_2026q2** all in a single pass. If we want to target only the parent without touching children, we use the new **ONLY** keyword.

In the following SQL block, we will explore both modes:

```
-- PostgreSQL 18 default: processes parent AND all children
VACUUM ANALYZE hr.attendance;


-- Target only the parent, skip children:
VACUUM ANALYZE ONLY hr.attendance;
```

Recipe #5: Implementing Automatic Partitioning

Manually creating partitions for each new time period is error-prone and operationally expensive. In this recipe, we automate partition creation using a PL/pgSQL function scheduled through **pg_cron**. This is needed so that our **sales.orders** table always has partitions ready for incoming data without manual intervention.

Create Automation Function

So, let us write a function that calculates the next month's date boundaries and creates a partition if one does not already exist. The function is idempotent, meaning it can be called repeatedly without causing errors if the partition has already been created.

With this in mind, we will now run the following SQL:

```
CREATE OR REPLACE FUNCTION sales.create_monthly_partition()
RETURNS void AS $$
DECLARE
    v_start DATE;
    v_end   DATE;
    v_name  TEXT;
BEGIN
    v_start := date_trunc('month', CURRENT_DATE) + INTERVAL '1
month';
    v_end   := v_start + INTERVAL '1 month';
    v_name  := 'orders_' || to_char(v_start, 'YYYYMM');

    -- Skip if partition already exists:
    IF EXISTS (
        SELECT 1 FROM pg_class
        WHERE relname = v_name
          AND relnamespace = 'sales'::regnamespace
    ) THEN
        RAISE NOTICE 'Partition % already exists, skipping.',
v_name;
        RETURN;
    END IF;

    EXECUTE format(
        'CREATE TABLE sales.%I PARTITION OF sales.orders
         FOR VALUES FROM (%L) TO (%L)',
        v_name, v_start, v_end
    );

    RAISE NOTICE 'Created partition sales.%', v_name;
```

```
END;
$$ LANGUAGE plpgsql;
```

Schedule with 'pg_cron'

We now proceed to install the **pg_cron** extension and schedule the function to run on the first day of each month:

```
CREATE EXTENSION IF NOT EXISTS pg_cron;

-- Schedule for the 1st of every month at midnight:
SELECT cron.schedule(
    'create-monthly-order-partition',
    '0 0 1 * *',
    'SELECT sales.create_monthly_partition()'
);
```

We can test the function immediately by calling it directly:

```
SELECT sales.create_monthly_partition();
```

The terminal will display a notice confirming the partition name. We will then verify the new partition exists by querying the catalog as we did in Recipe #3. This automation ensures we never encounter a "no partition for key" error when new orders arrive at the start of a month, and we can look ahead further by calling the function multiple times with adjusted **CURRENT_DATE** offsets if our workload requires several months of pre-provisioned partitions.

Recipe #6: Running Declarative Partitioning

Declarative partitioning, introduced in PostgreSQL 10 and refined in every subsequent release, is the recommended approach for most partitioning scenarios. It provides automatic tuple routing, partition pruning, and index propagation without requiring triggers or custom routing functions. In this recipe, we create a monthly partitioned **production.order_items** table with hash partitioning and demonstrate the PostgreSQL 18 relaxation that allows non-btree index types in unique constraints on partitioned tables.

Create Hash-Partitioned Table

We can now create a table to store individual line items for each order, distributing rows evenly across four partitions using hash partitioning on **`item_id`**. This strategy is ideal when there is no natural range or list attribute but we want to spread write load and vacuum work across multiple physical files.

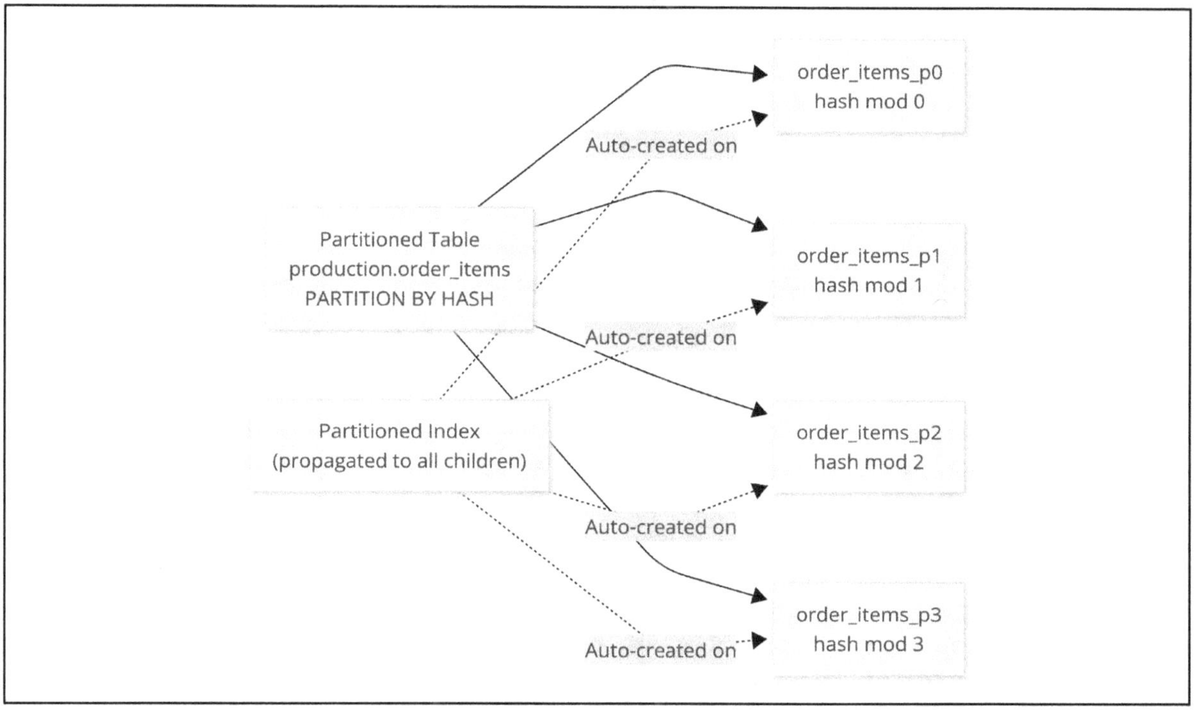

Fig 6.2: Declarative Partitioning Architecture

Following is how we do it:

```
CREATE TABLE production.order_items (
    item_id SERIAL,
    order_id INT NOT NULL,
    product_id INT NOT NULL REFERENCES
production.products(product_id),
    quantity INT DEFAULT 1,
    unit_price NUMERIC(10, 2),
    line_total NUMERIC(12, 2)
        GENERATED ALWAYS AS (quantity * unit_price),
    PRIMARY KEY (item_id)
) PARTITION BY HASH (item_id);
```

```
CREATE TABLE production.order_items_p0
    PARTITION OF production.order_items
    FOR VALUES WITH (MODULUS 4, REMAINDER 0);
CREATE TABLE production.order_items_p1
    PARTITION OF production.order_items
    FOR VALUES WITH (MODULUS 4, REMAINDER 1);
CREATE TABLE production.order_items_p2
    PARTITION OF production.order_items
    FOR VALUES WITH (MODULUS 4, REMAINDER 2);
CREATE TABLE production.order_items_p3
    PARTITION OF production.order_items
    FOR VALUES WITH (MODULUS 4, REMAINDER 3);
```

The **line_total** column uses the virtual generated column feature we configured in Chapter 2, demonstrating how PostgreSQL 18 features compose naturally with partitioning. The primary key on **item_id** alone (without including the partition key) works here because hash partitioning derives the partition from **item_id** itself, so local uniqueness within each hash bucket is sufficient to guarantee global uniqueness. We will then seed the table with sample data.

Following is the quick SQL query:

```
INSERT INTO production.order_items
    (order_id, product_id, quantity, unit_price)
SELECT
    (random() * 100 + 1)::int,
    p.product_id,
    (random() * 5 + 1)::int,
    p.list_price
FROM production.products p
CROSS JOIN generate_series(1, 10) AS g;
```

GiST and Non-Btree Indexes on Partitioned Tables

In previous PostgreSQL versions, unique constraints and primary keys on partitioned tables could only use B-tree indexes. PostgreSQL 18 relaxes this restriction, allowing GiST-based unique constraints to serve as partition keys, which is especially relevant for temporal constraints with **WITHOUT OVERLAPS** that we configured in Chapter 2. This means we can now create a partitioned table with a temporal primary key that enforces non-overlapping ranges per entity across partitions.

We try this by creating a partitioned version of the project assignments table:

```
CREATE TABLE hr.project_assignments_part (
    employee_id INT NOT NULL,
    project_name VARCHAR(100) NOT NULL,
    assignment_period daterange NOT NULL,
    assignment_year INT NOT NULL
        GENERATED ALWAYS AS
        (EXTRACT(YEAR FROM lower(assignment_period))::int) STORED,
    PRIMARY KEY (employee_id, assignment_period WITHOUT OVERLAPS)
) PARTITION BY LIST (assignment_year);

CREATE TABLE hr.proj_assign_2025
    PARTITION OF hr.project_assignments_part
    FOR VALUES IN (2025);
CREATE TABLE hr.proj_assign_2026
    PARTITION OF hr.project_assignments_part
    FOR VALUES IN (2026);
```

The **PRIMARY KEY (employee_id, assignment_period WITHOUT OVERLAPS)** uses a GiST index internally, which was not allowed on partitioned tables before PostgreSQL 18. The **assignment_year** column is a stored generated column (not virtual, because we need it as a partition key) that extracts the year from the range's lower bound. Each partition enforces the non-overlapping constraint within its year, and the list-based partitioning ensures that assignments are physically grouped by year for efficient lifecycle management.

This combination of temporal constraints, generated columns, and declarative partitioning is a powerful PostgreSQL 18 pattern that we can apply to any time-bounded entity in our application.

Recipe #7: Configuring Sharding with FDW and Citus

The partitioning distributes data across multiple files on a single server. And, sharding takes this further by distributing data across multiple independent servers, enabling horizontal scale-out for datasets that exceed the capacity of a single host. In this recipe, we configure manual sharding with Foreign Data Wrappers (FDW) for lightweight cross-server queries, and managed sharding with Citus for transparent distributed SQL.

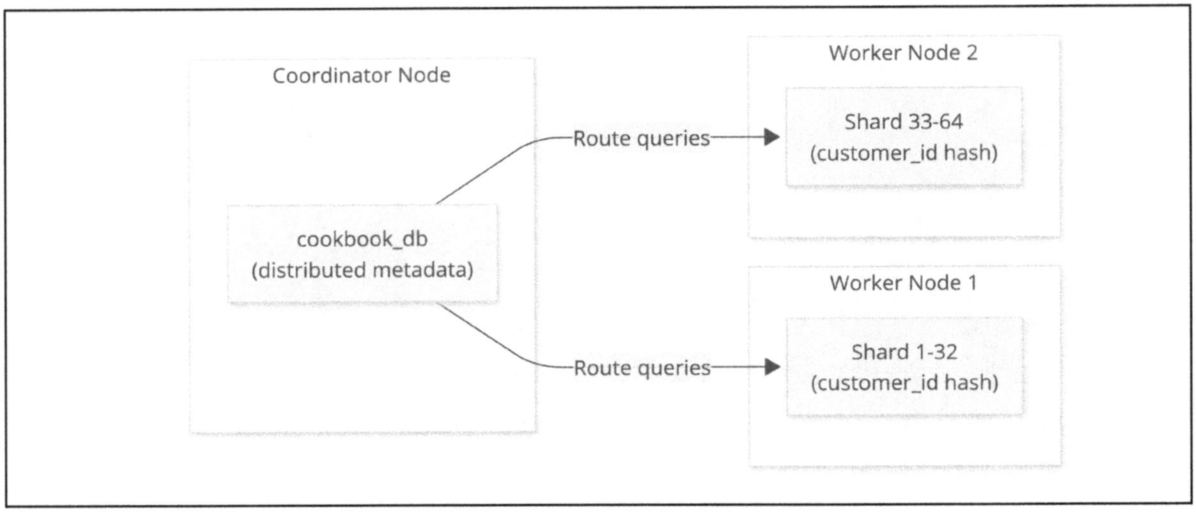

Fig 6.3: Sharding Architecture with Citus

Setup FDW-based Sharding

At this point, we will use the **postgres_fdw** extension (which ships with PostgreSQL and does not require external packages) to create foreign tables that point to partitions hosted on remote servers. This approach is lighter than Citus and suitable for read-heavy workloads where writes are routed to the appropriate shard at the application level. So here, we will create a shard map and foreign tables, then run the following SQL on the coordinator server:

```
CREATE EXTENSION IF NOT EXISTS postgres_fdw;

-- Define the remote shard server:
CREATE SERVER shard_node_1
    FOREIGN DATA WRAPPER postgres_fdw
    OPTIONS (host 'shard1.internal', port '5432',
             dbname 'cookbook_db');

-- Map local postgres role to remote credentials:
```

```
CREATE USER MAPPING FOR postgres
    SERVER shard_node_1
    OPTIONS (user 'postgres', password '<PASSWORD>');

-- Create a foreign table pointing to a remote partition:
CREATE FOREIGN TABLE sales.orders_shard1 (
    order_id INT,
    customer_name VARCHAR(100),
    employee_id INT,
    order_date DATE,
    total_due NUMERIC(12, 2),
    territory VARCHAR(50)
)
SERVER shard_node_1
OPTIONS (schema_name 'sales', table_name 'orders');
```

We can now query **sales.orders_shard1** as if it were local, and PostgreSQL pushes qualifying conditions and joins to the remote server, minimizing network data transfer. As we configured **mysql_fdw** in Chapter 4, the FDW pattern is familiar; the difference here is that we use **postgres_fdw** for PostgreSQL-to-PostgreSQL communication, which supports full pushdown of sorts, aggregates, joins, and UPDATE/DELETE operations.

Configure Sharding with Citus

For applications that require transparent distributed SQL with automatic shard routing, rebalancing, and distributed transactions, Citus provides a managed sharding layer on top of PostgreSQL. With this in mind, we will now install the Citus extension on the coordinator node and all worker nodes. We now proceed to run the following commands on each node:

```
sudo apt install -y postgresql-18-citus-13.0

# Add citus to shared_preload_libraries in postgresql.conf:
sudo nano /etc/postgresql/18/main/postgresql.conf
# shared_preload_libraries = 'citus'
```

```
sudo systemctl restart postgresql
```

On the coordinator node, we create the extension and register the worker nodes:

```
CREATE EXTENSION citus;

-- Register worker nodes:
SELECT citus_set_coordinator_host('coordinator.internal', 5432);
SELECT citus_add_node('worker1.internal', 5432);
SELECT citus_add_node('worker2.internal', 5432);

-- Distribute the orders table by a hash of customer_name:
SELECT create_distributed_table('sales.orders', 'customer_name');
```

After distribution, every **INSERT**, **SELECT**, **UPDATE**, and **DELETE** against **sales.orders** is transparently routed to the appropriate worker based on the hash of **customer_name**. Queries that filter on the distribution column run on a single shard, while cross-shard queries are parallelized across all workers and merged on the coordinator.

Here, we will verify the distribution by querying the Citus metadata:

```
SELECT nodename, count(*) AS shard_count
FROM citus_shards
GROUP BY nodename
ORDER BY nodename;
```

The output confirms that shards are evenly distributed across the two worker nodes. For production deployments, we should co-locate related tables (such as **production.order_items** and **sales.orders**) by distributing both on the same column to enable local joins within each shard. From here, we configure this using **create_distributed_table** with a matching distribution column on each related table, and Citus will co-locate shards automatically for efficient distributed joins.

Summary

This chapter transformed our **cookbook_db** from a collection of monolithic tables into a well-partitioned, scalable architecture. We replaced the flat **sales.orders** table with a range-partitioned structure and observed how PostgreSQL 18's improved partition pruning and partitionwise join support reduce query execution time by scanning only the relevant partitions. We applied vertical partitioning to the **production.products** table to isolate large, infrequently accessed columns, and we created a list-partitioned **production.inventory** table organized by warehouse location.

We practiced the full partition lifecycle through attach, detach, and drop operations, and we built inheritance-based partitioning for the **hr.attendance** table, noting the PostgreSQL 18 behavioral change where **VACUUM** and **ANALYZE** now recurse into child tables by default. We automated partition creation with a **pg_cron**-scheduled function that ensures monthly partitions are always pre-provisioned. In our declarative partitioning recipe, we demonstrated the PostgreSQL 18 relaxation that allows GiST-based unique constraints (including temporal **WITHOUT OVERLAPS** primary keys) on partitioned tables, combining temporal constraints, generated columns, and partitioning into a single powerful pattern.

Finally, we configured both FDW-based sharding for lightweight cross-server federation and Citus-based sharding for transparent distributed SQL with automatic shard routing and rebalancing.

CHAPTER 7

REPLICATION, SCALABILITY AND HIGH AVAILABILITY

Introduction

This chapter takes us through the replication and high availability infrastructure that transforms our **cookbook_db** from a single server into a resilient, horizontally scalable cluster. We will start by configuring physical streaming replication between a primary and a standby node using PostgreSQL 18's updated terminology and configuration defaults. From there, we will install and configure **repmgr** for automated cluster management and failover, clone databases across nodes, and deploy a Patroni-managed high availability cluster backed by **etcd**.

We will front the cluster with HAProxy for load balancing and **pgbouncer** for connection pooling, giving applications a single stable endpoint that survives node failures. We will then cover the process of upgrading a live replication cluster to PostgreSQL 18, taking advantage of the optimizer statistics preservation and parallel checks we covered in Chapter 4. Finally, we will configure the logical replication slot synchronization feature, enabling logical subscribers to seamlessly continue replicating after a physical standby is promoted to primary.

Every configuration file, SQL command, and monitoring query in this chapter operates against the **cookbook_db** database and the partitioned schemas we built across Chapters 1 through 6. We proceed to use Linux exclusively, and all paths reference the PostgreSQL 18 binary and data directory layout established in Chapter 1.

Recipe #1: Using Primary-Standby Replication

Physical streaming replication creates a byte-for-byte copy of the primary server on one or more standby nodes, providing both read scale-out and a warm failover target. Every WAL record generated on the primary is shipped to the standby in near-real time, keeping the two clusters synchronized. In this recipe, we configure streaming replication between two servers, i.e. one hosting **cookbook_db** primary and the other standby one capable of answering read queries.

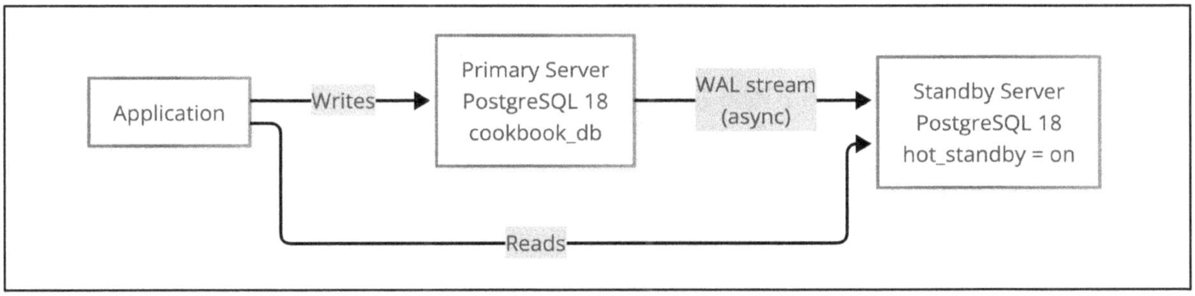

Fig 7.1: Primary-Standby Streaming Replication Architecture

Configure Primary Server

On the primary server, we open **postgresql.conf** and verify the replication parameters.

Most of these were configured in Chapter 5 for WAL management; here we add the replication-specific settings. So here, we will then add or modify the following lines:

```
wal_level = replica
max_wal_senders = 10
wal_keep_size = 256   # MB, retain WAL for standby reconnection
max_replication_slots = 10
```

We will then create a dedicated replication role with the **REPLICATION** privilege and a physical replication slot that ensures WAL retention for the standby.

For this, we will again connect to **cookbook_db** and run the following:

```
CREATE USER replication_user
    WITH REPLICATION ENCRYPTED PASSWORD 'repl_secure_pass';

SELECT * FROM pg_create_physical_replication_slot('standby_slot');
```

We then add an entry to **pg_hba.conf** that permits replication connections from the standby server using **scram-sha-256** authentication, which is the PostgreSQL default that replaced the deprecated **md5** method, as we configured in Chapter 1. We will now add the following line:

```
host replication replication_user <STANDBY_IP>/32 scram-sha-256
```

We restart the primary to apply the changes:

```
sudo systemctl restart postgresql
```

Setup Standby Server

On the standby server, we stop PostgreSQL (if running), remove any existing data directory contents, and use **pg_basebackup** to create a full copy of the primary. In the following commands, we will proceed:

```
sudo systemctl stop postgresql
sudo rm -rf /var/lib/postgresql/18/main/*

sudo -u postgres pg_basebackup \
    -h <PRIMARY_IP> -p 5432 \
```

```
    -U replication_user \
    -D /var/lib/postgresql/18/main \
    -P --slot=standby_slot \
    --write-recovery-conf

# Enable hot standby for read queries:
sudo -u postgres bash -c \
    "echo 'hot_standby = on' >>
/var/lib/postgresql/18/main/postgresql.conf"

sudo systemctl start postgresql
```

The **--write-recovery-conf** flag automatically creates the **standby.signal** file and populates **primary_conninfo** in **postgresql.conf**, telling PostgreSQL that this cluster should operate as a standby. Once started, the standby connects to the primary and begins streaming WAL.

So, let us verify replication from the primary:

```
SELECT client_addr, state, sent_lsn, write_lsn,
       flush_lsn, replay_lsn
FROM pg_stat_replication;
```

The output should show the standby's IP address with a **state** of **streaming**, confirming that WAL is flowing continuously.

Recipe #2: Installing and Configuring 'repmgr'

The **repmgr** tool automates PostgreSQL cluster management, handling node registration, cloning, failover, and monitoring through a unified command-line interface. In this recipe, we install **repmgr** on both the primary and standby nodes, register them into a managed cluster, and verify the cluster topology.

Install and Configure

With this in mind, we will now install the PostgreSQL repmgr package on both nodes. We now proceed to run the following commands on each server:

```
sudo apt update
```

```
sudo apt install -y postgresql-18-repmgr
```

On the primary node, we create the **repmgr** user and database:

```
CREATE USER repmgr WITH SUPERUSER LOGIN
    ENCRYPTED PASSWORD 'repmgr_secure_pass';
CREATE DATABASE repmgr WITH OWNER repmgr;
```

Here, we will create the **repmgr.conf** configuration file on the primary node at **/etc/repmgr.conf**. We can now write the following content:

```
node_id = 1
node_name = 'primary'
conninfo = 'host=<PRIMARY_IP> dbname=repmgr user=repmgr
           password=repmgr_secure_pass'
data_directory = '/var/lib/postgresql/18/main'
```

So here, we will then register the primary node and verify the cluster state:

```
sudo -u postgres repmgr -f /etc/repmgr.conf primary register
sudo -u postgres repmgr -f /etc/repmgr.conf cluster show
```

The cluster show output displays the primary node with a role of **primary** and a status of *** running**. We then configure the standby node's **repmgr.conf** with **node_id = 2** and **node_name = 'standby'**, register it using **repmgr standby register**, and verify that both nodes appear in the cluster show output. We refer to the repmgr documentation for advanced features such as automatic failover via **repmgrd**, event notification hooks, and witness nodes.

Verify Cluster State

After registering the primary node, we verify the full cluster state using both the repmgr CLI and PostgreSQL's built-in replication catalog. We run the following on the primary to get an instant picture of replication health across all connected nodes:

```
SELECT client_addr, state, sent_lsn,
       write_lsn, flush_lsn, replay_lsn,
       (sent_lsn - replay_lsn) AS replication_lag
FROM pg_stat_replication;
```

The pg_stat_replication view shows one row per connected standby, including the client address, replication state, and LSN positions for sent, written, flushed, and replayed WAL. The replication_lag column indicates how many bytes of WAL the standby has not yet applied, giving us an instant measure of replication health. A lag close to zero confirms synchronous or near-synchronous replication.

We keep this query ready throughout the high availability chapters that follow, as it is our primary tool for monitoring the repmgr-managed cluster and making informed decisions before any planned switchover or failover event.

Recipe #3: Cloning Database with 'repmgr'

The addition of a new standby to an existing repmgr-managed cluster requires cloning of the primary's data directory to the new node. The **`repmgr standby clone`** command handles this process, including base backup, recovery configuration, and slot setup, in a single command.

Clone and Register

On the new node, we configure **`repmgr.conf`** with a unique **`node_id`** and **`node_name`**. We then stop PostgreSQL, clone the primary, start the service, and register the new standby:

```
# On the new standby node:
sudo systemctl stop postgresql


sudo -u postgres repmgr \
    -h <PRIMARY_IP> \
    -f /etc/repmgr.conf \
    standby clone


sudo systemctl start postgresql


sudo -u postgres repmgr \
    -f /etc/repmgr.conf \
    standby register
```

We will now verify the expanded cluster by running the following command on any node:

```
sudo -u postgres repmgr -f /etc/repmgr.conf cluster show
```

The output now lists the primary and both standbys nodes. At this stage, we verify streaming replication health using the same **pg_stat_replication** query from Recipe #1, which should show two rows corresponding to the two standby connections. If we need to test failover, we promote one standby using **repmgr standby promote** and then rejoin the old primary as a standby using **repmgr standby follow**. The **repmgr** tool handles the **pg_rewind** operation automatically when **use_pg_rewind = true** is set in the configuration file.

Verify Streaming Replication Health

After registering the new standby with repmgr, we perform a deeper health check by querying pg_stat_replication on the primary to confirm the node is streaming actively. At this stage, we run the following query on the primary server to see all connected standbys and their current replication positions:

```
SELECT application_name, client_addr, state,
       sent_lsn, replay_lsn,
       (sent_lsn - replay_lsn) AS lag_bytes
FROM pg_stat_replication
ORDER BY client_addr;
```

Each row in the output represents one registered standby node. The state column should show streaming for a healthy standby that has caught up with the primary's WAL. A state of startup indicates the node is still replaying WAL from the base backup produced during cloning. The lag_bytes value expresses how far behind the standby is in bytes, which directly translates to the recovery point objective in a failover scenario.

We monitor this value continuously in production deployments to ensure our standbys always remain within an acceptable lag window before any planned switchover or unplanned failover event.

Recipe #4: Deploying High Availability Cluster with Patroni

Patroni automates PostgreSQL cluster management by coordinating leader election, replication configuration, and automatic failover through a distributed configuration store. Unlike **repmgr**, which relies on SSH-based health checks, Patroni uses **etcd**, Consul, or ZooKeeper to maintain consensus about cluster state, making it more resilient to network partitions. In this recipe, we deploy a two-node Patroni cluster backed by **etcd**.

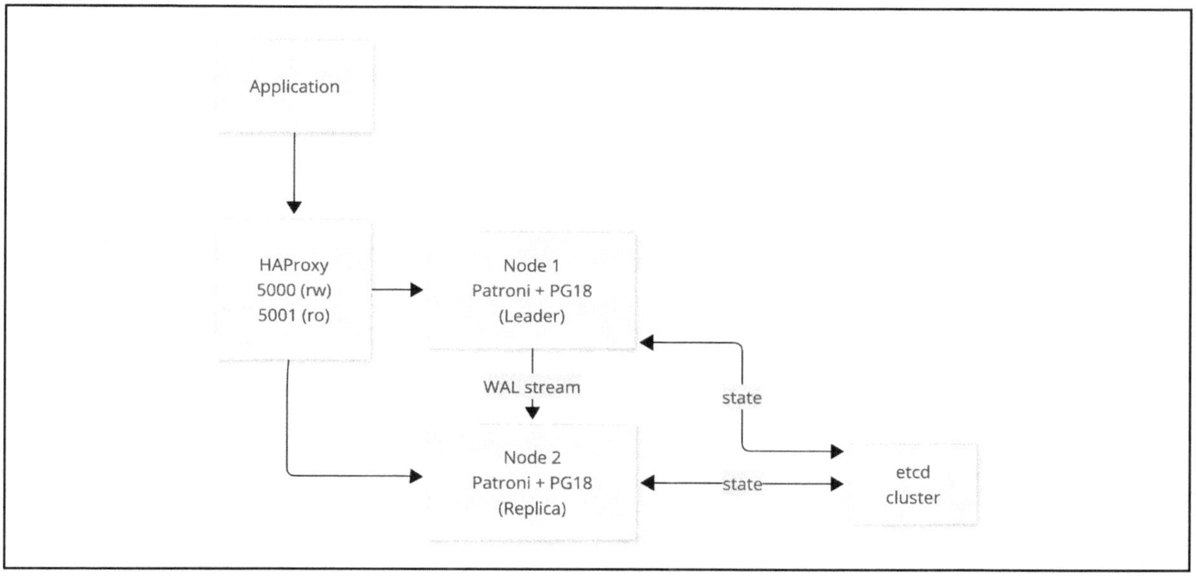

Fig 7.2: Patroni HA Cluster Architecture

Install and Configure etcd

At this point, we will install **etcd** on a dedicated server (or on one of the PostgreSQL nodes for development environments). In the following commands, we will proceed:

```
sudo apt update
sudo apt install -y etcd

# Edit /etc/default/etcd:
ETCD_LISTEN_CLIENT_URLS="http://0.0.0.0:2379"
ETCD_ADVERTISE_CLIENT_URLS="http://<ETCD_IP>:2379"

sudo systemctl restart etcd
sudo systemctl enable etcd

# Verify:
etcdctl endpoint health
```

Configure Patroni on Each Node

So, let us install Patroni on each PostgreSQL node:

```
sudo apt install -y python3-pip python3-venv
python3 -m venv /opt/patroni
source /opt/patroni/bin/activate
pip install patroni[etcd] psycopg2-binary
```

We now proceed to create the Patroni configuration file at **/etc/patroni.yml** on each node. The following shows the configuration for node 1; node 2 uses the same structure with its own IP address and **name** field:

```
scope: cookbook-cluster
namespace: /service/
name: node1

restapi:
  listen: 0.0.0.0:8008
  connect_address: <NODE1_IP>:8008

etcd:
  host: <ETCD_IP>:2379

bootstrap:
  dcs:
    ttl: 30
    loop_wait: 10
    retry_timeout: 10
    maximum_lag_on_failover: 1048576
    postgresql:
      use_pg_rewind: true
      parameters:
        wal_level: replica
        hot_standby: 'on'
```

```
      wal_keep_size: 256
      max_wal_senders: 10
      max_replication_slots: 10
  initdb:
    - encoding: UTF8
    - locale: en_US.UTF-8

postgresql:
  listen: 0.0.0.0:5432
  connect_address: <NODE1_IP>:5432
  data_dir: /var/lib/postgresql/18/main
  bin_dir: /usr/lib/postgresql/18/bin
  authentication:
    superuser:
      username: postgres
      password: pg_secure_pass
    replication:
      username: replicator
      password: repl_secure_pass
```

At this stage, we will then start Patroni on the first node. It initializes the PostgreSQL cluster and elects itself as leader. We then start Patroni on the second node, which clones from the leader automatically. Here, we will run the following command on each node:

```
sudo /opt/patroni/bin/patroni /etc/patroni.yml &
```

We can now verify the cluster state using the REST API. So here, we will then run the following command:

```
curl -s http://<NODE1_IP>:8008/cluster | python3 -m json.tool
```

The output lists both members with their roles (**leader** and **replica**), timeline IDs, and lag values. To test failover, we stop PostgreSQL on the leader node and observe Patroni automatically promoting the replica within the **ttl** window. After the old leader restarts, Patroni uses **pg_rewind** to rejoin it as a replica, restoring the two-node topology without manual intervention.

Recipe #5: Using HAProxy and PgBouncer for High Availability

Applications connecting directly to PostgreSQL nodes must implement their own failover logic, which is complex and error-prone. HAProxy provides a stable virtual IP that routes traffic to the current primary (for writes) or any healthy replica (for reads), while **pgbouncer** pools connections to reduce per-backend overhead. In this recipe, we deploy both tools in front of our Patroni-managed cluster, as we already configured **pgbouncer** in Chapter 3 for the RDS environment, here we adapt it for the on-premises cluster.

Configure HAProxy

We will then install HAProxy on a dedicated load-balancer node:

```
sudo apt update
sudo apt install -y haproxy
```

We edit **/etc/haproxy/haproxy.cfg** to define separate frontends for read-write and read-only traffic, using Patroni's REST API health checks to route correctly. We will now add the following configuration:

```
frontend pg_write
    bind *:5000
    mode tcp
    default_backend pg_primary

frontend pg_read
    bind *:5001
    mode tcp
    default_backend pg_replicas

backend pg_primary
    mode tcp
    option httpchk GET /primary
    http-check expect status 200
    default-server inter 3s fall 3 rise 2
```

```
    server node1 <NODE1_IP>:5432 check port 8008
    server node2 <NODE2_IP>:5432 check port 8008

backend pg_replicas
    mode tcp
    option httpchk GET /replica
    http-check expect status 200
    balance roundrobin
    default-server inter 3s fall 3 rise 2
    server node1 <NODE1_IP>:5432 check port 8008
    server node2 <NODE2_IP>:5432 check port 8008

listen stats
    bind *:8404
    stats enable
    stats uri /
    stats refresh 5s
```

The health checks query Patroni's REST API on port **`8008`**. The **`/primary`** endpoint returns **`200`** only on the leader node, so that the writes go to the current primary. The **`/replica`** endpoint returns **`200`** on standby nodes, distributing read traffic via round-robin. We restart HAProxy and test connectivity.

At this point, we will run the following codeblock:

```
sudo systemctl restart haproxy

# Test write endpoint:
psql -h <HAPROXY_IP> -p 5000 -U postgres -d cookbook_db \
    -c "SELECT pg_is_in_recovery();"

# Test read endpoint:
psql -h <HAPROXY_IP> -p 5001 -U postgres -d cookbook_db \
    -c "SELECT pg_is_in_recovery();"
```

The write endpoint returns **f** (not in recovery, meaning it is the primary), while the read endpoint returns **t** (in recovery, meaning it is a standby). After a failover, HAProxy automatically redirects traffic to the new primary within the **inter** check interval, providing seamless connectivity for applications using the stable **<HAPROXY_IP>:5000** write endpoint. So here, we configure **pgbouncer** on the same host or each application server, pointing it to the HAProxy endpoints.

As we covered the **pgbouncer** configuration details in Chapter 3 Recipe #4, we refer back to that recipe for the **pgbouncer.ini** setup and instead focus here on verifying end-to-end connectivity through the application to **pgbouncer** to HAProxy to PostgreSQL.

Install and Configure PgBouncer

HAProxy routes connections at the TCP level to the correct PostgreSQL node, but each connection still opens a dedicated backend process on the server, consuming memory and CPU. We now layer PgBouncer on top of HAProxy to provide connection pooling, reducing the number of live backend processes regardless of how many application clients connect simultaneously. We install PgBouncer on the same load-balancer node where HAProxy is already running:

```
sudo apt install -y pgbouncer
```

We configure /etc/pgbouncer/pgbouncer.ini to forward application connections from port 6432 to HAProxy's write endpoint on port 5000. We now add the following settings to the configuration file:

```
[databases]
cookbook_db = host=127.0.0.1 port=5000 dbname=cookbook_db

[pgbouncer]
listen_addr       = 0.0.0.0
listen_port       = 6432
auth_type         = scram-sha-256
auth_file         = /etc/pgbouncer/userlist.txt
pool_mode         = transaction
max_client_conn   = 500
default_pool_size = 20
```

The transaction pool mode releases a server connection back to the pool after every transaction, which is the most efficient pooling strategy for typical OLTP workloads. We set max_client_conn to 500 to accommodate all application threads, while default_pool_size limits active backend connections to 20 per database. We then add our database user to /etc/pgbouncer/userlist.txt and restart the service.

Recipe #6: Performing Database Upgrade on Replication Cluster

Do you know, that the upgradation of a replication cluster to PostgreSQL 18 requires the upgrade to be co-ordinated across all nodes while minimizing downtime. The strategy is to upgrade the primary first, then rebuild or upgrade each standby. As we covered the standalone **pg_upgrade** workflow in Chapter 4 Recipe #7, this recipe focuses on sequencing the upgrade across nodes, rebuilding standbys from the upgraded primary, and verifying replication health after the upgrade.

Upgrade Primary Node

We begin by taking a full backup of the entire cluster using **pg_dumpall** as a safety net. In the following command, we will on the primary:

```
pg_dumpall -h <PRIMARY_IP> -U postgres > full_cluster_backup.sql
```

We then follow the **pg_upgrade** process from Chapter 4 Recipe #7. As we covered in that recipe, PostgreSQL 18's **pg_upgrade** preserves optimizer statistics automatically and runs compatibility checks in parallel, so we do not repeat those steps here. After starting the upgraded primary, we run the post-upgrade statistics fill-in:

```
sudo -u postgres /usr/lib/postgresql/18/bin/vacuumdb \
    --all --analyze-in-stages --missing-stats-only --jobs=4
```

With this in place, we verify the primary is operational by connecting to **cookbook_db** and running **SELECT version()** to confirm the PostgreSQL version string appears.

Rebuild Standby Nodes

After the primary is upgraded and running, each standby must be rebuilt from the new primary. The most reliable approach is to use **pg_basebackup** to create a fresh base backup from the upgraded primary, exactly as we did in Recipe #1 of this chapter. With this in mind, we will now run the following commands on each standby node:

```
sudo systemctl stop postgresql
sudo rm -rf /var/lib/postgresql/18/main/*


sudo -u postgres pg_basebackup \
```

```
    -h <PRIMARY_IP> -p 5432 \
    -U replication_user \
    -D /var/lib/postgresql/18/main \
    -P --slot=standby_slot \
    --write-recovery-conf

sudo systemctl start postgresql
```

After each standby starts, we verify replication health using the **pg_stat_replication** query from Recipe #1. All standby nodes should show a **state** of **streaming** with minimal lag. If we are using Patroni (as configured in Recipe #4), the standby rebuilds happen automatically when Patroni detects the version mismatch and triggers a re-clone from the upgraded leader, requiring no manual intervention beyond the initial leader upgrade.

Recipe #7: Synchronizing Logical Replication Slots for Failover

In production deployments, logical replication subscribers consume a change stream from a publisher (primary) server. If the publisher fails and a physical standby is promoted, the subscriber must reconnect to the new primary and resume the change stream without losing any events. Before PostgreSQL 17, this required complex manual slot manipulation on the standby after promotion. PostgreSQL 17 introduced **sync_replication_slots** to automate this process, and PostgreSQL 18 refines it with the **pg_createsubscriber** utility and improved slot synchronization reliability.

In this recipe, we configure logical replication slot synchronization so that our **cookbook_db** logical subscribers survive a physical failover transparently.

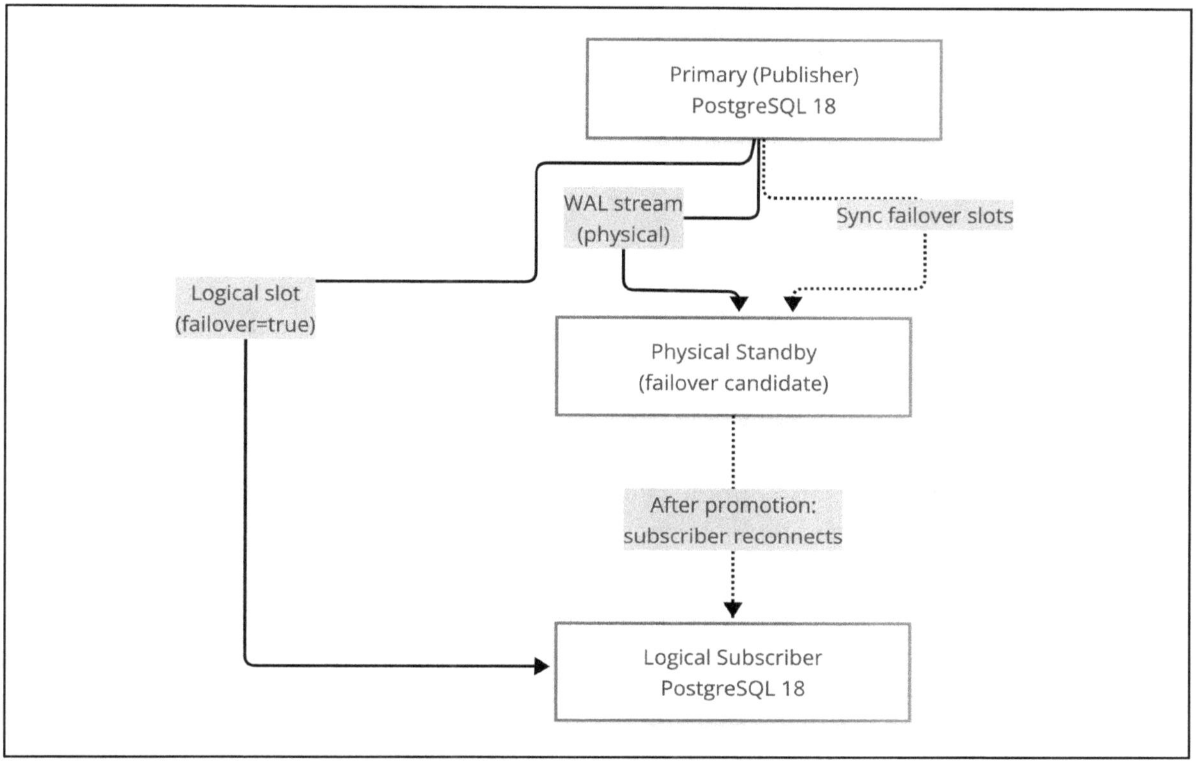

Fig 7.3: Logical Replication Slot Failover Architecture

Configure Publisher and Subscription

On the primary server (the publisher), we create a publication that covers the tables in our **cookbook_db** that we want to replicate logically:

```
-- On the PRIMARY (publisher):
CREATE PUBLICATION cookbook_pub
    FOR TABLE hr.employees, sales.orders, production.products;
```

On a separate PostgreSQL server acting as the logical subscriber, we create a subscription with the **failover = true** option. This flag tells the publisher to mark the underlying replication slot as failover-eligible, which enables slot synchronization to physical standbys. At this stage, we will then run the following SQL on the subscriber:

```
-- On the SUBSCRIBER:
CREATE SUBSCRIPTION cookbook_sub
    CONNECTION 'host=<PRIMARY_IP> port=5432
```

```
                dbname=cookbook_db user=postgres
                password=pg_secure_pass'
    PUBLICATION cookbook_pub
    WITH (failover = true);
```

Here, we will verify that the slot was created with failover enabled on the publisher. We can now run the following SQL on the primary:

```
SELECT slot_name, slot_type, failover
FROM pg_replication_slots
WHERE slot_type = 'logical';
```

The output should show the subscription's slot with **failover = t**, confirming that this slot is eligible for synchronization to physical standbys.

```
  slot_name   | slot_type | failover
-------------+-----------+----------
 cookbook_sub | logical   | t
(1 row)
```

Enable Slot Synchronization on Standby

On the physical standby (our failover candidate from Recipe #1), we enable automatic slot synchronization by setting **sync_replication_slots = on** in **postgresql.conf**. We also configure **synchronized_standby_slots** on the primary to prevent the logical subscriber from consuming changes before the standby has received them, which guarantees that no events are lost during failover. So here, we will then configure the following settings:

```
# On the STANDBY (postgresql.conf):
sync_replication_slots = on

# On the PRIMARY (postgresql.conf):
synchronized_standby_slots = 'standby_slot'
```

We restart both the primary and the standby to apply these changes. The standby's slot synchronizer process will now periodically copy the failover-eligible logical slots from the primary, keeping them current so that a promoted standby can immediately serve the subscriber's replication stream. We will then verify synchronization by querying the standby's

pg_replication_slots view:

```
SELECT slot_name, synced,
       (synced AND NOT temporary
        AND invalidation_reason IS NULL) AS failover_ready
FROM pg_replication_slots;
```

The output must show **synced = t** and **failover_ready = t** for the **cookbook_sub** slot. If **synced** is **f**, we check the standby log for synchronization errors, which typically indicate that the primary's WAL retention is insufficient or that **hot_standby_feedback** is not enabled. We can also trigger a manual synchronization to diagnose issues. We will now run the following SQL on the standby:

```
SELECT pg_sync_replication_slots();
```

Test Failover

To validate the complete failover flow, we simulate a primary failure by stopping PostgreSQL on the primary and promoting the standby. If we are using Patroni (Recipe #4), the promotion happens automatically.

So, for a manual test, we run the following commands:

```
# Stop the primary:
sudo systemctl stop postgresql


# Promote the standby:
sudo -u postgres pg_ctl promote \
    -D /var/lib/postgresql/18/main
```

After promotion, the subscriber must update its connection to point to the newly promoted server. At this point, we will run the following SQL on the subscriber:

```
ALTER SUBSCRIPTION cookbook_sub
    CONNECTION 'host=<NEW_PRIMARY_IP> port=5432
               dbname=cookbook_db user=postgres
               password=pg_secure_pass';
```

The subscription resumes replicating from exactly the LSN where the old primary left off, with no data loss, because the synced slot on the promoted standby maintained the same position as the original slot on the old primary.

SO now, we will verify that the subscriber is actively replicating by running the following SQL on the new primary:

```
SELECT slot_name, active, confirmed_flush_lsn
FROM pg_replication_slots
WHERE slot_name = 'cookbook_sub';
```

The **active = t** value confirms that the subscriber has reconnected and is consuming the change stream from the promoted standby. This entire failover process, from primary failure to subscriber reconnection, takes only seconds in a Patroni-managed environment, making logical replication viable for production deployments that require high availability on both the publisher and subscriber sides of the pipeline.

Component	Configuration	Purpose
Publisher (Primary)	CREATE PUBLICATION ... FOR TABLE	Define which tables to replicate logically
Subscriber	CREATE SUBSCRIPTION ... WITH (failover = true)	Mark the slot as failover-eligible
Primary	synchronized_standby_slots = 'standby_slot'	Prevent subscriber from advancing past standby
Standby	sync_replication_slots = on	Enable automatic slot synchronization
Subscriber (post-failover)	ALTER SUBSCRIPTION ... CONNECTION ...	Redirect to the promoted standby

Summary

This chapter transformed our single-server **cookbook_db** into a resilient, horizontally scalable cluster with automated failover and logical replication continuity. We configured physical streaming replication between a primary and standby using PostgreSQL 18's default **scram-sha-256** authentication, then layered **repmgr** on top for automated node registration, cloning, and failover management. We deployed a Patroni cluster backed by **etcd** for consensus-based leader election and automatic failover, and fronted the cluster with HAProxy for connection routing and **pgbouncer** for connection pooling, giving applications a single stable endpoint that survives node failures.

We covered the process of upgrading the entire replication cluster to PostgreSQL 18, referencing the **pg_upgrade** workflow from Chapter 4 for the primary upgrade and using **pg_basebackup** to rebuild standbys from the upgraded primary. Most significantly, we configured the logical replication slot synchronization feature so that logical subscribers survive physical failover transparently. By creating subscriptions with **failover = true**, enabling **sync_replication_slots** on the standby, and setting **synchronized_standby_slots** on the primary, we established a pipeline where a promoted standby can immediately serve the subscriber's change stream without data loss.

CHAPTER 8

BLOB, JSON QUERY, RETURNING CLAUSE AND CONNECTIONS

Introduction

This chapter takes us through the advanced data type operations and SQL capabilities that round out our day-to-day work with the **cookbook_db** application. We will start by importing binary large objects using the **bytea** data type and a Python helper script, adding product image storage to our **production** schema. We will then automate SQL operations through shell scripts, building reusable command-line tools that connect to **cookbook_db** and execute queries as part of scheduled workflows. We will work with PostgreSQL's JSONB data type to store, query, update, and index semi-structured data within our **sales** schema. We will also practice the **CAST** operator and the **::** shorthand to transform data types across queries, inserts, and filters.

Beyond these foundational techniques, this chapter introduces two headline PostgreSQL 18 features that directly improve how we capture and generate data. The new **OLD** and **NEW** aliases in **RETURNING** clauses allow us to access both the previous and current state of a row within a single **INSERT**, **UPDATE**, **DELETE**, or **MERGE** statement, eliminating the need for separate **SELECT** queries or trigger-based audit trails. The new **uuidv7()** function generates time-ordered UUIDs that sort chronologically, making them ideal for primary keys in distributed systems where both uniqueness and temporal ordering are required.

Recipe #1: Importing BLOB Data Types

Binary Large Objects (BLOBs) store files such as images, PDFs, and audio clips directly inside the database using the **bytea** data type. In this recipe, we add a product images table to our **production** schema and import binary files using a Python helper script that converts raw bytes to the hex-encoded format PostgreSQL requires for **bytea** inserts.

Create Storage Table and Import Data

So, let us create a table in the **production** schema to store product images alongside a reference to the **products** table we built in Chapter 2. With this in mind, we will now connect to **cookbook_db** and run the following SQL:

```
CREATE TABLE production.product_images (
    image_id SERIAL PRIMARY KEY,
    product_id INT REFERENCES production.products(product_id),
    file_name VARCHAR(255) NOT NULL,
    file_data BYTEA NOT NULL,
    uploaded_at TIMESTAMPTZ DEFAULT now()
    );
```

Before we can insert a binary file, we must convert it to a hex-encoded string. We now proceed to create a Python helper script named **blob_import.py** that reads a file and outputs the hex representation. At this stage, we will then create the following file:

```
#!/usr/bin/env python3
"""Convert a binary file to a hex string for bytea insertion."""
import sys


def convert_to_hex(file_path: str) -> str:
    with open(file_path, 'rb') as f:
        return '\\x' + f.read().hex()


if __name__ == '__main__':
    if len(sys.argv) != 2:
        print('Usage: python3 blob_import.py <file_path>')
        sys.exit(1)
    print(convert_to_hex(sys.argv[1]))
```

Here, we will run the script against a sample product image file to generate the hex string:

```
python3 blob_import.py /home/ubuntu/images/bike_pro.jpg >
/tmp/hex_output.txt
```

We then insert the hex-encoded data into the database. In a production workflow, we would wrap this in a parameterized query using **psycopg** or a similar driver to avoid shell escaping issues. For our demonstration, we use the **psql \lo_import** alternative or a direct **INSERT** with the hex string. So here, we will then run the following SQL, replacing the hex placeholder with the actual output from the script:

```
INSERT INTO production.product_images (product_id, file_name,
file_data)
VALUES (1, 'bike_pro.jpg', E'\\x<HEX_STRING_FROM_SCRIPT>');
```

We will then verify the import by querying the table and checking the stored file size:

```
SELECT image_id, product_id, file_name,
       pg_size_pretty(length(file_data)::bigint) AS file_size,
       uploaded_at
```

```
FROM production.product_images;
```

The output shows the image file name, its byte-level size, and the upload timestamp. To convert the stored data back to a binary file, we use a complementary Python script that reads the hex string from a query result and writes the original bytes to disk. This round-trip capability is essential for applications that serve binary content directly from the database, such as product catalogs or document management systems.

Export and Retrieve BLOB Data

We now retrieve the stored BLOB and reconstruct the original binary file using a Python script that reads the bytea column and writes it back to disk. At this stage, we will then create a companion script named blob_export.py that reverses the import process we completed in the first subsection:

```
#!/usr/bin/env python3
"""Retrieve a bytea column from PostgreSQL and write it to a
file."""
import psycopg, sys


def export_blob(image_id: int, output_path: str) -> None:
    conn_str = 'dbname=cookbook_db user=postgres host=localhost'
    with psycopg.connect(conn_str) as conn:
        with conn.cursor() as cur:
            cur.execute(
                'SELECT file_name, file_data FROM
production.product_images'
                ' WHERE image_id = %s', (image_id,)
            )
            row = cur.fetchone()
            if row:
                file_name, file_data = row
                with open(output_path or file_name, 'wb') as f:
                    f.write(bytes(file_data))
                print(f'Exported {file_name} to {output_path}')
```

```
if __name__ == '__main__':
    export_blob(int(sys.argv[1]), sys.argv[2] if len(sys.argv) > 2
else None)
```

We run this script by providing the image_id and the destination file path. The script connects to cookbook_db, fetches the bytea column, and writes the raw bytes directly to the output file. This round-trip approach, importing with blob_import.py and exporting with blob_export.py, gives us a complete binary asset management workflow for the production schema.

As our cookbook_db application expands in later chapters, we will wrap these operations in parameterized queries, add transaction-level error handling, and apply the pgAudit configuration from Chapter 9 to log every import and export operation for compliance purposes.

Recipe #2: Running Queries using Shell

When we automate the SQL execution through shell scripts, it integrates the PostgreSQL operations into cron jobs, CI/CD pipelines, and monitoring workflows. In this recipe, we create a reusable shell script that connects to our **cookbook_db** instance, executes one or more SQL queries, and handles errors gracefully.

Create Shell Script

We will now create a new file named **cookbook_query.sh** that parameterizes the connection details and accepts SQL as an argument or from a file. At this point, we will write the following content:

```
touch ~/cookbook_query.sh
chmod +x ~/cookbook_query.sh
```

We will then open the file and add the following script:

```
#!/bin/bash

# Connection parameters for cookbook_db
DB_NAME="cookbook_db"
DB_USER="postgres"
DB_HOST="localhost"
DB_PORT="5432"
```

```
# Accept a SQL string as argument or default query
QUERY="${1:-SELECT version();}"

# Use .pgpass or PGPASSWORD for authentication
export PGPASSWORD="${PGPASSWORD:?Set PGPASSWORD before running}"

# Execute the query with error handling
if ! psql -h "$DB_HOST" -p "$DB_PORT" -U "$DB_USER" \
          -d "$DB_NAME" -c "$QUERY"; then
    echo "ERROR: Query execution failed." >&2
    unset PGPASSWORD
    exit 1
fi

unset PGPASSWORD
```

So, let us test the script by passing a query that retrieves employee data from our **hr** schema. With this in mind, we will now run the following:

```
PGPASSWORD=pg_secure_pass ./cookbook_query.sh \
    "SELECT employee_id, full_name, salary FROM hr.employees;"
```

The script prints the result set to the terminal. If the connection or query fails, the error handler prints a message to **stderr** and exits with code **1**, which allows upstream tooling (such as cron or a CI pipeline) to detect the failure and trigger alerts. We can extend this script to accept a **.sql** file as input by replacing **-c "$QUERY"** with **-f "$1"**, enabling batch execution of multi-statement migration scripts.

Schedule with cron

We schedule the script to run a nightly summary query and write the output to a log file. We now proceed to open the crontab and add the following entry:

```
crontab -e

# Add the following line for a nightly 2:00 AM sales summary:
```

```
0 2 * * * PGPASSWORD=pg_secure_pass \
    /home/ubuntu/cookbook_query.sh \
    "SELECT territory, sum(total_due) FROM sales.orders GROUP BY
territory;" \
    >> /var/log/cookbook_nightly.log 2>&1
```

Recipe #3: Working with PostgreSQL JSON Data

PostgreSQL's **JSONB** data type stores semi-structured data in a binary format that supports indexing, containment checks, and path-based queries. In this recipe, we add a **JSONB** metadata column to our **sales.orders** table to capture order-level attributes that vary across transactions, such as payment method, shipping preferences, and discount codes.

Add and Populate JSONB Data

At this stage, we will then add a **metadata** column to the **sales.orders** table. Because this table is partitioned (as we configured in Chapter 6), the column addition propagates to all partition children automatically with the following query:

```
ALTER TABLE sales.orders ADD COLUMN metadata JSONB;


-- Populate with sample semi-structured data:
UPDATE sales.orders
SET metadata = jsonb_build_object(
    'payment_method', CASE (order_id % 3)
        WHEN 0 THEN 'credit_card'
        WHEN 1 THEN 'bank_transfer'
        ELSE 'upi'
    END,
    'shipping', jsonb_build_object(
        'method', 'express',
        'tracking_id', 'TRK-' || order_id
    ),
    'discount_code', CASE WHEN order_id % 5 = 0 THEN 'SAVE10' ELSE
NULL END
```

```
)
WHERE metadata IS NULL;
```

Query, Filter, and Index JSONB Data

We can now use PostgreSQL's JSON operators to extract, filter, and update values. The **->>** operator extracts a value as text, the **->** operator returns a JSON sub-object, and the **@>** operator tests containment. So here, we will then run the following SQL to demonstrate each pattern:

```
-- Extract a scalar value as text:
SELECT order_id, metadata->>'payment_method' AS payment
FROM sales.orders
WHERE metadata->>'payment_method' = 'upi'
LIMIT 5;

-- Navigate nested objects:
SELECT order_id,
       metadata->'shipping'->>'tracking_id' AS tracking
FROM sales.orders
WHERE metadata->'shipping'->>'method' = 'express'
LIMIT 5;

-- Containment check:
SELECT order_id, metadata->>'discount_code' AS discount
FROM sales.orders
WHERE metadata @> '{"discount_code": "SAVE10"}'::jsonb;

-- Update a nested value:
UPDATE sales.orders
SET metadata = jsonb_set(metadata, '{shipping,method}',
'"standard"')
WHERE order_id = 1;
```

```
-- Create a GIN index for fast containment queries:
CREATE INDEX idx_orders_metadata ON sales.orders USING GIN
(metadata);
```

The GIN index accelerates **@>** containment queries and **?** key-existence checks across the entire JSONB document, regardless of nesting depth. As we covered in Chapter 2 Recipe #3, PostgreSQL 18 builds GIN indexes in parallel by default, so the index creation command above will use multiple workers on tables with significant row counts, reducing build time substantially compared to earlier versions.

Recipe #4: Working with PostgreSQL CAST Operator

The **CAST** operator and its **::** shorthand convert values between data types within SQL statements. Type conversion is essential when comparing columns of different types, inserting string literals into numeric columns, or formatting timestamps for display. In this recipe, we apply casting across queries, inserts, updates, and filters using our **cookbook_db** tables.

Common Casting Patterns

We demonstrate the most frequently used casting scenarios against our **sales.orders** and **hr.employees** tables by running the following SQL:

```
-- Cast numeric to integer (truncate decimal):
SELECT order_id, total_due, total_due::INTEGER AS truncated_total
FROM sales.orders LIMIT 5;

-- Cast string literal to numeric during insert:
INSERT INTO sales.orders
    (customer_name, employee_id, order_date, total_due, territory)
VALUES ('CastDemo Corp', 1, CURRENT_DATE,
        CAST('4250.99' AS NUMERIC(12,2)), 'South Asia');

-- Cast timestamp to date in a WHERE filter:
SELECT order_id, customer_name, order_date
FROM sales.orders
WHERE order_date::DATE = '2025-07-01';
```

```
-- Cast integer to text for string concatenation:
SELECT 'Order #' || order_id::TEXT AS order_label,
       customer_name
FROM sales.orders LIMIT 5;

-- Cast JSONB value to integer for comparison:
SELECT order_id
FROM sales.orders
WHERE (metadata->>'discount_code') IS NOT NULL
  AND total_due::INTEGER > 1000;
```

The **::** shorthand is the idiomatic PostgreSQL form and is functionally identical to the standard SQL **CAST(expr AS type)** syntax. We prefer the shorthand throughout our **cookbook_db** codebase for readability, but both forms are valid and produce identical query plans. When casting between incompatible types, PostgreSQL will raise a runtime error; for example, casting a non-numeric string to **INTEGER** will fail, so we must ensure that source data is clean or use **CASE** expressions to handle edge cases before casting.

Handle Cast Failures Safely

We now address a common production hazard, which is a CAST operation that fails at runtime because the source value cannot be converted to the target type. In standard SQL, a failed cast raises an error that aborts the current transaction. PostgreSQL does not include a built-in TRY_CAST function, but we can implement equivalent safe-casting behavior using a user-defined function that traps the exception and returns NULL instead of propagating an error.

So here, we will now create a reusable helper function in the public schema:

```
CREATE OR REPLACE FUNCTION public.try_cast_numeric(v TEXT)
RETURNS NUMERIC AS $$
BEGIN
    RETURN v::NUMERIC;
EXCEPTION WHEN OTHERS THEN
    RETURN NULL;
END;
$$ LANGUAGE plpgsql IMMUTABLE STRICT;
```

The function attempts the cast inside a PL/pgSQL exception block and returns NULL if the conversion fails, leaving the rest of the transaction intact.

Recipe #5: Using OLD and NEW in RETURNING Clauses

PostgreSQL 18 introduces **OLD** and **NEW** aliases in the **RETURNING** clause of **INSERT**, **UPDATE**, **DELETE**, and **MERGE** statements. Previously, **RETURNING** could only surface one set of values, i.e. **INSERT** and **UPDATE** returned new values, while **DELETE** returned old values. If we needed to compare before-and-after states, we had to run separate **SELECT** queries, implement triggers, or manage change tracking at the application level. The **OLD** and **NEW** aliases eliminate that overhead by exposing both the pre-modification and post-modification row within a single atomic operation.

In this recipe, we apply this capability to track salary changes, audit order deletions, and detect upsert outcomes in our **cookbook_db** application.

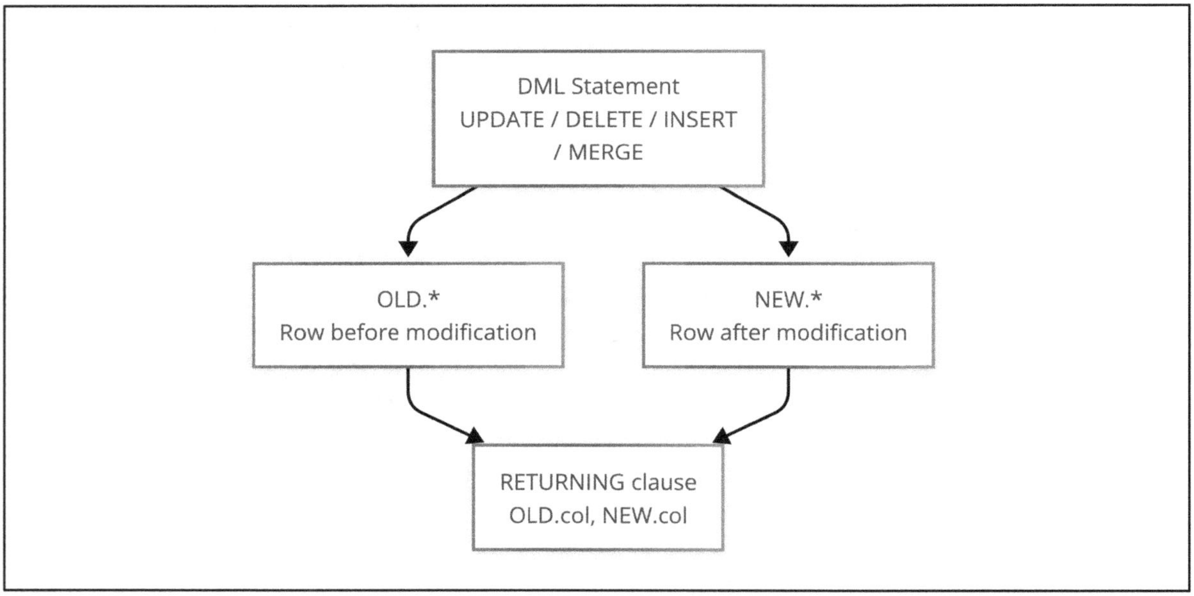

Fig 8.1: OLD/NEW RETURNING Data Flow

Track Salary Changes with UPDATE RETURNING

Let us now update an employee's salary and use the **RETURNING** clause with **OLD** and **NEW** to capture both the previous and updated values in a single statement with the following query:

```
UPDATE hr.employees
```

```
SET salary = 105000.00
WHERE employee_id = 1
RETURNING
    employee_id,
    OLD.salary  AS previous_salary,
    NEW.salary  AS updated_salary,
    NEW.salary - OLD.salary AS salary_change;
```

The terminal will then display the following output:

```
 employee_id | previous_salary | updated_salary | salary_change
-------------+-----------------+----------------+--------------
           1 |        98000.00 |      105000.00 |       7000.00
(1 row)
```

In a single round trip, we executed the salary update and received both the old and new values along with the computed difference. Without **OLD** and **NEW**, this would have required a **SELECT** before the **UPDATE** to capture the original salary, then the **UPDATE** itself, and optionally another **SELECT** to confirm the new value. The **OLD** alias provides the row as it existed before the modification, and **NEW** provides the row after, including any default recalculations or trigger-generated values.

The virtual generated column **annual_bonus** that we added in Chapter 2 will also reflect the new salary in the **NEW** alias automatically.

Audit Deletions with DELETE RETURNING

When we delete rows from our **sales.orders** table, we can capture the deleted data for audit purposes in the same statement. The **OLD** alias contains the row values at the moment of deletion, while **NEW** will be **NULL** since no row exists after a delete.

So here, we will run the following query:

```
DELETE FROM sales.orders
WHERE customer_name = 'CastDemo Corp'
RETURNING
    OLD.order_id,
    OLD.customer_name,
    OLD.total_due,
```

```
    OLD.order_date;
```

The result set returns the complete details of every deleted row, which we can pipe into an audit log table, a message queue, or an application-level change feed. This pattern eliminates the need for **BEFORE DELETE** triggers that copy rows to a shadow table, reducing both schema complexity and per-operation overhead.

Detect Upsert Outcomes with INSERT ON CONFLICT

When using **INSERT ... ON CONFLICT DO UPDATE** (an upsert), the **OLD** alias contains the conflicting row's values if a conflict occurred, or **NULL** if the row was freshly inserted. This allows us to determine the outcome of the upsert without additional queries. In the following SQL block, we will:

```
INSERT INTO production.products
    (product_name, product_number, category, list_price)
VALUES
    ('Mountain Bike Pro', 'MB-PRO-100', 'Bikes', 2699.99)
ON CONFLICT (product_number)
DO UPDATE SET list_price = EXCLUDED.list_price
RETURNING
    product_number,
    OLD.list_price AS was_price,
    NEW.list_price AS now_price,
    (OLD IS NULL)::boolean AS is_new_insert;
```

If the product already existed, **was_price** shows the original price and **is_new_insert** returns **false**. If the product was freshly inserted, **OLD** is entirely **NULL** and **is_new_insert** returns **true**. This pattern is invaluable for applications that need to distinguish between inserts and updates in upsert workflows, such as inventory synchronization or configuration management systems.

DML Operation	OLD Contains	NEW Contains
INSERT (no conflict)	NULL	Inserted row
INSERT ON CONFLICT DO UPDATE	Conflicting row before update	Row after update
UPDATE	Row before modification	Row after modification
DELETE	Row before deletion	NULL
MERGE (insert action)	NULL	Inserted row
MERGE (update action)	Row before modification	Row after modification
MERGE (delete action)	Row before deletion	NULL

Recipe #6: Generating Time-Ordered UUIDs

PostgreSQL 18 adds the **uuidv7()** function, which generates Version 7 UUIDs as defined in RFC 9562. Unlike the traditional **gen_random_uuid()** function (which produces Version 4 UUIDs with fully random bits), **uuidv7()** embeds a millisecond-precision Unix timestamp in the most significant 48 bits of the UUID. This design guarantees that UUIDs generated later will sort after those generated earlier, making them ideal for primary keys on tables where chronological ordering matters, such as event logs, audit trails, and distributed message queues.

The embedded timestamp also improves B-tree index performance by reducing page splits that occur when random UUIDs are inserted into an ordered index.

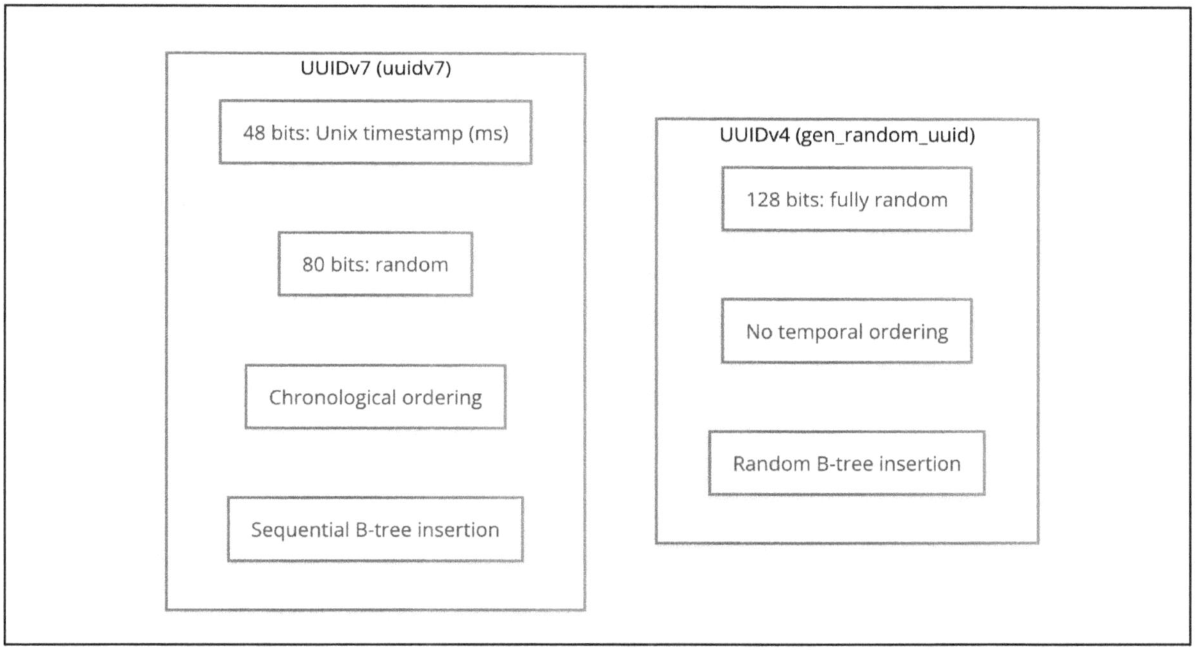

Fig 8.2: UUIDv4 vs UUIDv7 Structure Comparison

Using 'uuidv7()' as Primary Key

So, let us create an event log table in our **cookbook_db** that uses **uuidv7()** as the default primary key generator. This table will serve as the audit destination for the change tracking patterns we demonstrated in Recipe #5. With this in mind, we will now run the following query:

```
CREATE TABLE public.event_log (
    event_id UUID PRIMARY KEY DEFAULT uuidv7(),
```

```
    event_type VARCHAR(50) NOT NULL,
    entity_schema VARCHAR(50),
    entity_table VARCHAR(50),
    entity_id INT,
    payload JSONB,
    created_at TIMESTAMPTZ DEFAULT now()
    );
```

We now proceed to insert several events and observe that the generated UUIDs sort chronologically:

```
INSERT INTO public.event_log (event_type, entity_schema,
    entity_table, entity_id, payload)
VALUES
    ('salary_update', 'hr', 'employees', 1,
     '{"old_salary": 98000, "new_salary": 105000}'),
    ('order_created', 'sales', 'orders', 101,
     '{"customer": "TechCorp India", "total": 15200}'),
    ('product_price_change', 'production', 'products', 1,
     '{"old_price": 2499.99, "new_price": 2699.99}');

SELECT event_id, event_type, created_at
FROM public.event_log
ORDER BY event_id;
```

The terminal will display following similar output:

```
               event_id               |     event_type      |
created_at
--------------------------------------+---------------------+------
-------------------------
 019663a1-2b40-7000-8a1c-3d4e5f6a7b8c | salary_update       | 2026-
04-25 10:15:22.140+05:30
 019663a1-2b41-7000-9c2d-4e5f6a7b8c9d | order_created       |
2026-04-25 10:15:22.141+05:30
```

```
 019663a1-2b42-7000-ae3e-5f6a7b8c9d0e | product_price_change |
2026-04-25 10:15:22.142+05:30
```

The UUIDs are visually sortable by their leading hex characters, which encode the timestamp. The first 12 hex characters (**019663a1-2b40**, **019663a1-2b41**, **019663a1-2b42**) increment with each millisecond, confirming chronological ordering. The digit **7** in the third group identifies these as Version 7 UUIDs per the RFC 9562 specification.

Extract Timestamp from UUIDv7

Because the timestamp is embedded in the UUID itself, we can extract the creation time directly from the identifier without querying a separate **created_at** column. Here, we will write a SQL expression that extracts the millisecond-precision timestamp:

```
SELECT event_id,
       to_timestamp(
           ('x' || replace(
               left(event_id::text, 13), '-', ''
           ))::bit(48)::bigint / 1000.0
       ) AS embedded_timestamp
FROM public.event_log
ORDER BY event_id;
```

The extracted timestamps match the **created_at** values, confirming that the UUID encodes the event time accurately. This technique is useful for forensic analysis, debugging distributed systems, and verifying that event arrived in the expected order. In applications where storage efficiency matters, we can even omit the **created_at** column entirely and derive it from the UUID on read, saving 8 bytes per row.

UUIDv4 vs UUIDv7 Performance

On B-tree indexes, Version 4 UUIDs cause random insertions across the entire index tree because their values are uniformly distributed. This pattern generates frequent page splits and cache misses, degrading insert throughput as the table grows. Version 7 UUIDs, by contrast, insert sequentially at the rightmost leaf of the B-tree (the most recent timestamp), which is the same access pattern as **SERIAL** or **BIGSERIAL** columns. The result is fewer page splits, better cache locality, and higher sustained insert throughput.

For our **event_log** table, which will accumulate rows over the lifetime of the application, **uuidv7()** provides the uniqueness guarantees of a UUID with the insert performance characteristics of a sequential integer. We will use this **event_log** table as the audit destination throughout the remaining chapters, feeding it from the **OLD/NEW RETURNING** patterns we built in Recipe #5.

Summary

This chapter extended our **cookbook_db** application with advanced data type handling and two significant PostgreSQL 18 SQL enhancements. We stored binary product images using the **bytea** data type with a Python hex-encoding helper, automated SQL execution through a reusable shell script integrated with cron, and worked extensively with **JSONB** data including insertion, nested queries, containment checks, updates via **jsonb_set**, and GIN indexing. We practiced the **CAST** operator and **::** shorthand across a range of type conversion scenarios.

The two new recipes in this chapter introduce capabilities that fundamentally simplify change tracking and key generation in PostgreSQL 18. The **OLD** and **NEW** aliases in **RETURNING** clauses give us before-and-after visibility in a single **UPDATE**, **DELETE**, **INSERT**, or **MERGE** statement, eliminating the need for triggers, shadow tables, or separate **SELECT** queries when building audit trails. The **uuidv7()** function generates time-ordered UUIDs that combine the uniqueness of random identifiers with the sequential insert performance of integer keys, making them the preferred choice for primary keys on tables that accumulate data over time. Together, these features enabled us to create the **public.event_log** table that will serve as our centralized audit destination throughout the remaining chapters.

CHAPTER 9
AUTHENTICATION, AUDIT AND ENCRYPTION

Introduction

This chapter covers the security infrastructure that protects our **cookbook_db** application at every layer, including role management, encrypted connections, data-at-rest encryption, audit logging, directory-based authentication, and the two headline security features introduced in PostgreSQL 18. We will manage roles and permissions using **scram-sha-256** authentication (which PostgreSQL 18 mandates as the default over the now-deprecated **md5** method), configure SSL certificates for encrypted client-server communication, implement at-rest encryption with OpenSSL, deploy **pgAudit** alongside trigger-based audit logging, and integrate LDAP for centralized directory authentication.

We will then set up the native OAuth 2.0 authentication that PostgreSQL 18 introduces via the SASL **OAUTHBEARER** mechanism, enabling our database to authenticate users with bearer tokens issued by external identity providers such as Keycloak, Auth0, or Azure AD. Finally, we will migrate existing **md5**-authenticated roles to **scram-sha-256** before the deprecated method is removed in a future release.

Every configuration change and SQL command in this chapter operates against the **cookbook_db** database, the roles we create here, and the schemas we built across Chapters 1 through 8. We now proceed to reference the SSL and connection setup from Chapter 1 and the **pgbouncer** configuration from Chapter 3 where applicable, avoiding repetition of steps already covered.

Recipe #1: Manage Permission, Authentication and Authorization

PostgreSQL roles serve as both users and groups, providing a flexible security model where permissions are granted to roles and roles are granted to other roles. In this recipe, we create application roles for our **cookbook_db**, assign schema-level permissions, configure **scram-sha-256** authentication in **pg_hba.conf**, and highlight a PostgreSQL 18 behavioral change affecting **AFTER** triggers and role context.

Create Roles and Manage Membership

So here, we will then create a **hr_manager** role for the **hr** schema, a **sales_analyst** role for read-only access to **sales** data, and a **prod_admin** role for the **production** schema. We then create individual login users and assign them to these roles. We will then connect as the **postgres** superuser and run the following SQL:

```
-- Create group roles (no LOGIN):
CREATE ROLE hr_manager NOLOGIN;
```

```
CREATE ROLE sales_analyst NOLOGIN;
CREATE ROLE prod_admin NOLOGIN;

-- Create login users with scram-sha-256 passwords:
CREATE USER anika WITH PASSWORD 'anika_secure_pass';
CREATE USER rohan WITH PASSWORD 'rohan_secure_pass';
CREATE USER priya WITH PASSWORD 'priya_secure_pass';

-- Assign users to group roles:
GRANT hr_manager TO anika;
GRANT sales_analyst TO rohan;
GRANT prod_admin TO priya;

-- Grant schema-level permissions to group roles:
GRANT USAGE ON SCHEMA hr TO hr_manager;
GRANT SELECT, INSERT, UPDATE, DELETE ON ALL TABLES IN SCHEMA hr
    TO hr_manager;

GRANT USAGE ON SCHEMA sales TO sales_analyst;
GRANT SELECT ON ALL TABLES IN SCHEMA sales TO sales_analyst;

GRANT USAGE ON SCHEMA production TO prod_admin;
GRANT ALL PRIVILEGES ON ALL TABLES IN SCHEMA production
    TO prod_admin;
```

Configure Authentication in 'pg_hba.conf'

Let us now open **pg_hba.conf** and replace any legacy **md5** entries with **scram-sha-256**, which is the PostgreSQL default. The **md5** method is now deprecated and will emit warnings in the server log (controlled by the new **md5_password_warnings** parameter, which we will cover in Recipe #7). We will now configure the following entries:

```
# Local connections:
```

```
local   all   all                                        scram-sha-256

# Remote connections from our application subnet:
host    all   all   192.168.1.0/24                       scram-sha-256

# SSL-only connections for admin roles:
hostssl all   postgres   0.0.0.0/0                       scram-sha-256
```

We restart the service to apply the authentication changes:

```
sudo systemctl restart postgresql
```

AFTER Trigger Role Behavior Change

PostgreSQL 18 changes the role context in which **AFTER** triggers execute. In previous versions, an **AFTER** trigger ran as the role active at the time of **COMMIT**, which could differ from the role that performed the original **INSERT**, **UPDATE**, or **DELETE** if a **SET ROLE** statement was executed between the DML operation and the commit.

In PostgreSQL 18, **AFTER** triggers now execute as the role that was active at the time the trigger event was queued (the time of the DML statement), regardless of any subsequent **SET ROLE** calls within the same transaction. This change improves security by checking that audit triggers always captures the identity of the user who performed the modification, not a potentially different role that was assumed later in the transaction. Our audit trigger from Chapter 8 (which we will extend in Recipe #4) benefits from this change automatically, as **current_user** inside the trigger function now always reflects the originating role.

Recipe #2: Setting up SSL Authentication

SSL encrypts the connection between client and server, protecting credentials and data in transit from network-level interception. As we configured the basic **listen_addresses** and **pg_hba.conf** entries in Chapter 1, we focus here on generating the certificate infrastructure and verifying encrypted connections. We will use self-signed certificates for our **cookbook_db** environment; production deployments should use certificates from a trusted Certificate Authority.

Generate Certificates and Configure PostgreSQL

To generate a self-signed certificate and private key using OpenSSL, we will run the following:

```
sudo openssl req -new -x509 -days 365 -nodes \
```

```
    -out /etc/postgresql/18/main/server.crt \
    -keyout /etc/postgresql/18/main/server.key \
    -subj '/CN=cookbook-pg18'

sudo chown postgres:postgres \
    /etc/postgresql/18/main/server.crt \
    /etc/postgresql/18/main/server.key
sudo chmod 600 /etc/postgresql/18/main/server.key
```

With this in mind, we will now enable SSL in **postgresql.conf** by adding the following settings:

```
ssl = on
ssl_cert_file = '/etc/postgresql/18/main/server.crt'
ssl_key_file = '/etc/postgresql/18/main/server.key'
```

We restart the service and verify that SSL connections are active:

```
sudo systemctl restart postgresql

psql "postgresql://anika@localhost/cookbook_db?sslmode=require" \
    -c "SELECT ssl, version FROM pg_stat_ssl WHERE pid =
pg_backend_pid();"
```

The output confirms that the connection is encrypted with TLS. The **sslmode=require** parameter forces the client to use SSL, and any attempt to connect without encryption will be rejected by the **hostssl** entry in **pg_hba.conf**. For production environments, we would distribute a CA certificate to clients using the **sslrootcert** connection parameter and set **sslmode=verify-full** to validate the server's identity.

Enforce Client Certificate Authentication

We now extend SSL to require mutual authentication, where clients must present a certificate signed by our CA in addition to the server presenting its own certificate. This bidirectional verification prevents unauthorized clients from connecting even when they know the database credentials. We first generate a client certificate for our anika user. We run the following commands on the database server to create the key, the signing request, and the signed certificate in a single sequence:

```
sudo openssl genrsa -out /tmp/anika.key 2048
sudo openssl req -new -key /tmp/anika.key \
    -out /tmp/anika.csr -subj '/CN=anika'
sudo openssl x509 -req -in /tmp/anika.csr \
    -CA /etc/postgresql/18/main/server.crt \
    -CAkey /etc/postgresql/18/main/server.key \
    -CAcreateserial -out /tmp/anika.crt -days 365
```

We then configure pg_hba.conf to require a valid client certificate for connections to cookbook_db by adding the clientcert parameter. We update the existing SSL host entry as follows:

```
hostssl  cookbook_db  anika  0.0.0.0/0  scram-sha-256
clientcert=verify-full
```

The verify-full option instructs PostgreSQL to validate the client certificate against the server's CA certificate and verify that the certificate CN field matches the connecting database username. After restarting the server, the anika user must supply both a valid SCRAM password and a signed certificate to establish a connection. Any attempt using only a password is rejected with an SSL certificate verification failure. This two-factor authentication model significantly raises the bar for unauthorized access and is commonly required in PCI-DSS and SOC 2 compliant deployment environments.

Recipe #3: Configure Encryption with OpenSSL

While SSL protects data in transit, encryption at rest protects database files on disk against unauthorized access in scenarios such as disk theft, decommissioned hardware, or compromised backup media. In this recipe, we use OpenSSL to encrypt a database export and demonstrate the encrypt-decrypt workflow that safeguards our **cookbook_db** backups. For full Transparent Data Encryption (TDE), production deployments typically use filesystem-level encryption such as LUKS on Linux or cloud-provided disk encryption (AWS EBS encryption, for example), as PostgreSQL does not natively encrypt individual data files at rest.

Encrypt Database Exports

At this stage, we will then generate a 256-bit AES encryption key and use it to encrypt a **pg_dump** archive of our **cookbook_db**:

```
# Generate a random encryption key:
```

```
openssl rand -out /root/cookbook_encryption.key 32
chmod 600 /root/cookbook_encryption.key

# Create a dump and encrypt it:
sudo -u postgres pg_dump -F c cookbook_db \
    > /tmp/cookbook_db.dump

openssl enc -aes-256-cbc -salt -pbkdf2 \
    -in /tmp/cookbook_db.dump \
    -out /tmp/cookbook_db.dump.enc \
    -pass file:/root/cookbook_encryption.key

# Securely remove the unencrypted dump:
shred -u /tmp/cookbook_db.dump
```

The encrypted file **cookbook_db.dump.enc** can now be safely stored on backup media, transferred over untrusted networks, or archived in S3 alongside the WAL archives we configured in Chapter 5.

Decrypt and Restore Database

To restore from the encrypted backup, we reverse the process as shown below:

```
# Decrypt:
openssl enc -d -aes-256-cbc -pbkdf2 \
    -in /tmp/cookbook_db.dump.enc \
    -out /tmp/cookbook_db_restored.dump \
    -pass file:/root/cookbook_encryption.key

# Restore:
sudo -u postgres pg_restore \
    -d cookbook_db_restore \
    /tmp/cookbook_db_restored.dump
```

The encryption key file must be stored securely, ideally in a hardware security module (HSM), a secrets manager such as HashiCorp Vault, or an AWS KMS-managed key. If the key is lost, the encrypted backup becomes permanently unrecoverable. For filesystem-level encryption on our Linux server, we would configure LUKS on the partition that hosts the PostgreSQL data directory, which is transparent to the database process and does not require any changes to **postgresql.conf**.

Recipe #4: Implementing Audit Logging with 'pgAudit' and Triggers

Audit logging provides a tamper-evident record of who accessed or modified data, when the change occurred, and what the change contained. In this recipe, we install **pgAudit** for session-level and object-level audit logging, and we extend the trigger-based audit mechanism to feed our **public.event_log** table from Chapter 8.

Install and Configure 'pgAudit'

So here, we will then install the PostgreSQL pgAudit package and enable the extension:

```
sudo apt install -y postgresql-18-pgaudit
```

Let us now add **pgaudit** to **shared_preload_libraries** in **postgresql.conf** and configure the audit scope. We will now add the following settings:

```
shared_preload_libraries = 'pgaudit'
pgaudit.log = 'ddl, write'
pgaudit.log_relation = on
pgaudit.log_parameter = on
```

We then restart the service, and enable the extension in **cookbook_db**:

```
CREATE EXTENSION pgaudit;
```

With these settings, every DDL statement (**CREATE**, **ALTER**, **DROP**) and every write operation (**INSERT**, **UPDATE**, **DELETE**) generates a log entry in the PostgreSQL server log prefixed with **AUDIT:**. The **log_relation** option includes the specific table name in each entry, and **log_parameter** logs the bound parameter values, providing a complete picture of every modification. We can filter audit entries from the server log. In the following command, we will:

```
sudo grep AUDIT /var/log/postgresql/postgresql-18-main.log | tail -
10
```

Extend Trigger-Based Audit to 'event_log'

So, let us build on the trigger-based audit approach from the second edition by connecting it to the **public.event_log** table we created in Chapter 8 with **uuidv7()** primary keys. With this in mind, we will now create a generic audit trigger function that logs changes from any table into **event_log**.

```
CREATE OR REPLACE FUNCTION public.audit_to_event_log()
RETURNS TRIGGER AS $$
BEGIN
    IF TG_OP = 'DELETE' THEN
        INSERT INTO public.event_log
            (event_type, entity_schema, entity_table, payload)
        VALUES
            (TG_OP, TG_TABLE_SCHEMA, TG_TABLE_NAME,
             row_to_json(OLD)::jsonb);
        RETURN OLD;
    ELSIF TG_OP = 'UPDATE' THEN
        INSERT INTO public.event_log
            (event_type, entity_schema, entity_table, payload)
        VALUES
            (TG_OP, TG_TABLE_SCHEMA, TG_TABLE_NAME,
             jsonb_build_object(
                 'old', row_to_json(OLD)::jsonb,
                 'new', row_to_json(NEW)::jsonb));
        RETURN NEW;
    ELSIF TG_OP = 'INSERT' THEN
        INSERT INTO public.event_log
            (event_type, entity_schema, entity_table, payload)
        VALUES
            (TG_OP, TG_TABLE_SCHEMA, TG_TABLE_NAME,
             row_to_json(NEW)::jsonb);
        RETURN NEW;
```

```
    END IF;
    RETURN NULL;
END;
$$ LANGUAGE plpgsql;
```

We attach this trigger to our most sensitive tables. At this stage, we will then run the following SQL:

```
CREATE TRIGGER trg_audit_employees
    AFTER INSERT OR UPDATE OR DELETE ON hr.employees
    FOR EACH ROW EXECUTE FUNCTION public.audit_to_event_log();

CREATE TRIGGER trg_audit_orders
    AFTER INSERT OR UPDATE OR DELETE ON sales.orders
    FOR EACH ROW EXECUTE FUNCTION public.audit_to_event_log();
```

Every change to **hr.employees** and **sales.orders** now generates a row in **public.event_log** with a time-ordered **uuidv7()** identifier, the operation type, the schema and table name, and the full before/after payload. Because of the PostgreSQL 18 **AFTER** trigger role fix we covered in Recipe #1, the **current_user** recorded by this trigger always reflects the user who performed the DML operation, not a role assumed later in the transaction.

Recipe #5: Installing and Configuring LDAP Authentication

LDAP authentication delegates user verification to a centralized directory service such as OpenLDAP or Microsoft Active Directory, eliminating the need to manage passwords in PostgreSQL's catalog. In this recipe, we configure our **cookbook_db** server to authenticate users against an OpenLDAP directory.

Configure LDAP Client and 'pg_hba.conf'

Here, we will install the LDAP client utilities on the PostgreSQL server:

```
sudo apt install -y ldap-utils
```

So here, we will then configure the LDAP client by editing **/etc/ldap/ldap.conf** with the base DN and server URI for our directory. We will then add the following content:

```
BASE    dc=techparts,dc=io
URI     ldap://ldap.techparts.io
```

Let us now add an LDAP authentication entry to **pg_hba.conf** for users connecting from the application subnet:

```
host  all  all  192.168.1.0/24  ldap
    ldapserver=ldap.techparts.io
    ldapport=389
    ldapprefix="uid="
    ldapsuffix=",ou=users,dc=techparts,dc=io"
```

We restart PostgreSQL and test the connection using LDAP credentials:

```
sudo systemctl restart postgresql

psql -h localhost -U anika -d cookbook_db
```

When **anika** connects, PostgreSQL constructs the DN **uid=anika,ou=users,dc=techparts,dc=io** and performs a simple bind against the LDAP server to verify the password. If the bind succeeds, the connection proceeds with whatever PostgreSQL role matches the username. In the following script, we will verify successful LDAP authentication by checking the server log for entries that confirm the LDAP bind:

```
sudo tail -5 /var/log/postgresql/postgresql-18-main.log
```

Test and Troubleshoot LDAP Connections

We now validate our LDAP integration by performing a test bind using the ldapsearch utility before attempting a full PostgreSQL connection. This step confirms that the directory server is reachable and that our LDAP configuration is correct, isolating connectivity problems before they surface as cryptic authentication errors in the PostgreSQL log.

```
ldapsearch -x -H ldap://ldap.techparts.io \
    -b 'ou=users,dc=techparts,dc=io' \
    -D 'uid=anika,ou=users,dc=techparts,dc=io' \
    -w '<ANIKA_LDAP_PASSWORD>' \
    '(uid=anika)'
```

A successful result returns the LDAP entry for anika with a result code of 0. If the search fails, we verify that the ldapserver, ldapport, ldapprefix, and ldapsuffix values in pg_hba.conf match the directory server's actual schema. Common problems include a mismatched base DN, a firewall blocking port 389, or an incorrectly formatted DN template. We then review the PostgreSQL server log for LDAP-specific diagnostic messages by filtering the log file using the following command, which surfaces authentication-related lines without exposing raw passwords:

```
sudo grep -i 'ldap\|authentication failed\|FATAL' \
    /var/log/postgresql/postgresql-18-main.log | tail -20
```

Recipe #6: Implementing OAuth 2.0 Authentication

PostgreSQL 18 introduces native OAuth 2.0 authentication via the SASL **OAUTHBEARER** mechanism. Instead of passwords, clients present bearer tokens issued by an external identity provider (IdP) such as Keycloak, Auth0, Google Workspace, or Azure AD. PostgreSQL validates these tokens through a pluggable validator module, then maps the authenticated identity to a database role. This approach eliminates static database passwords entirely for token-authenticated connections, centralizes identity management in the organization's existing SSO infrastructure, and enables short-lived, automatically rotated credentials.

In this recipe, we configure OAuth authentication for our **cookbook_db** server using a generic OIDC-compatible identity provider.

Prerequisites and Build Requirements

OAuth support requires PostgreSQL 18 compiled with **--with-openssl** and **--with-libcurl**. If we installed from the PGDG binary packages (as in Chapter 1 Recipe #2), these dependencies are included by default. If we compiled from source (Chapter 1 Recipe #3), we must add **--with-libcurl** to the **./configure** command and install the **libcurl4-openssl-dev** package. We also need an OAuth validator module, which is a shared library that PostgreSQL loads to verify tokens.

There are several open-source validators available for common IdPs. For this recipe, we assume a validator library named **oauth_jwt_validator** that performs offline JWT validation against the IdP's public keys.

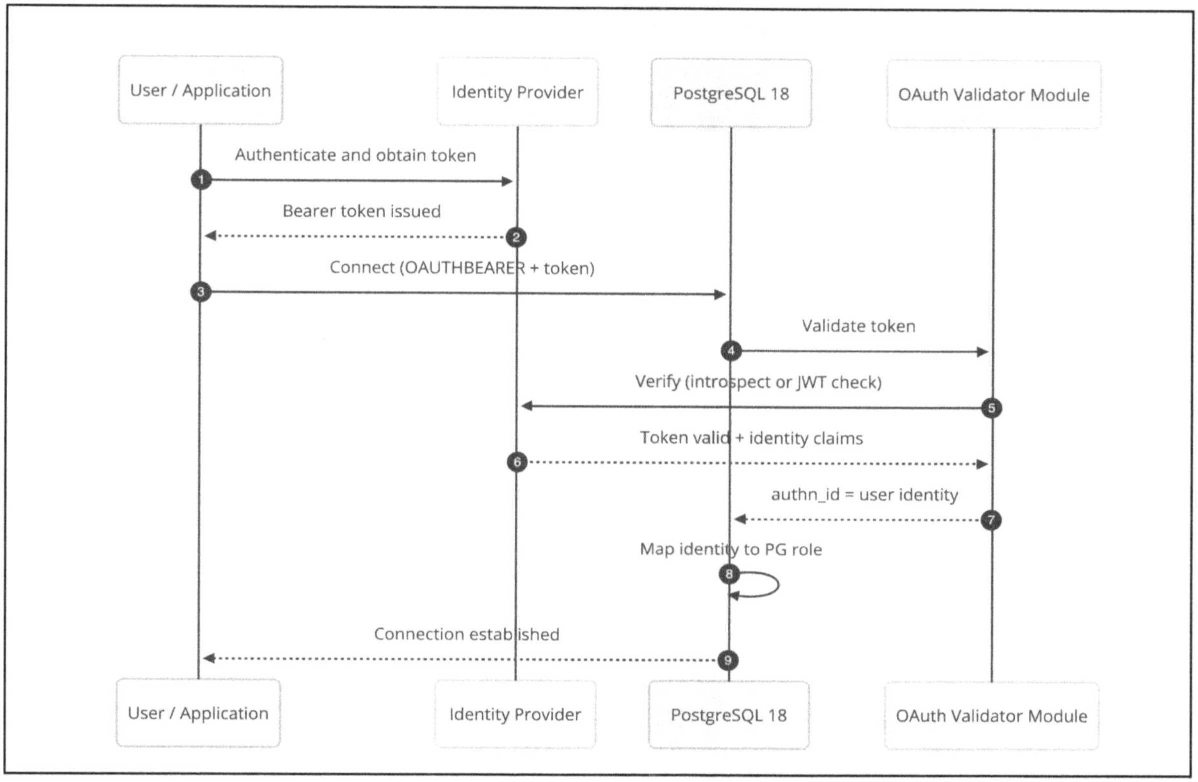

Fig 9.1: OAuth 2.0 Authentication Flow for PostgreSQL 18

Configure 'pg_hba.conf' for OAuth

With this in mind, we will now add an OAuth authentication entry to **pg_hba.conf** that specifies the IdP issuer URL, the required scope, and the validator library. We now proceed to add the following entry:

```
# OAuth authentication for application connections:
hostssl  cookbook_db  all  0.0.0.0/0  oauth
    issuer="https://auth.techparts.io/realms/cookbook"
    scope="openid"
    map=oauth_map
```

The **issuer** URL must match exactly the issuer identifier in the IdP's OIDC discovery document (**/.well-known/openid-configuration**). The **scope** parameter specifies which OAuth scopes the token must contain. The **map=oauth_map** parameter tells PostgreSQL to use a mapping defined in **pg_ident.conf** to translate OAuth identities to database roles. We need the **hostssl** prefix because **OAUTHBEARER** tokens are transmitted in cleartext within the SASL exchange and must be protected by TLS.

Map OAuth Identities to Database Roles

We edit **pg_ident.conf** to create the **oauth_map** that translates IdP usernames (typically the **sub** or **email** claim from the JWT) to PostgreSQL role names. At this stage, we will then add the following entries:

```
# MAPNAME       OAUTH-IDENTITY                    PG-ROLE
oauth_map       anika.sharma@techparts.io         anika
oauth_map       rohan.desai@techparts.io          rohan
oauth_map       priya.nair@techparts.io           priya
```

Here, we will configure the validator library in **postgresql.conf**. We can now add the following setting:

```
oauth_validator_libraries = 'oauth_jwt_validator'
```

We restart the service to apply all changes:

```
sudo systemctl restart postgresql
```

Connect using OAuth

With **psql** version 18 or later, we can connect using OAuth by specifying the **oauth_issuer** and **oauth_client_id** connection parameters. The **psql** client will initiate the Device Authorization flow, displaying a URL and a code that the user enters in a browser to authenticate with the IdP:

```
psql "host=pg.techparts.io port=5432 dbname=cookbook_db \
      user=anika sslmode=require \
      oauth_issuer=https://auth.techparts.io/realms/cookbook \
      oauth_client_id=cookbook-pg-client"
```

The terminal will display a device authorization prompt:

```
Visit https://auth.techparts.io/realms/cookbook/device
and enter the code: ABCD-EFGH
Waiting for authorization...
```

After we authorize in the browser, **psql** receives the bearer token and completes the SASL

OAUTHBEARER exchange with the server. The validator module verifies the token against the IdP's public keys, extracts the user identity (for example, **anika.sharma@techparts.io**), and PostgreSQL maps it to the **anika** role via **pg_ident.conf**. For applications that already possess a token (such as microservices using the client credentials grant), the token can be passed directly in the connection string or via the **PGOAUTH_BEARER_TOKEN** environment variable, bypassing the interactive device flow entirely.

Recipe #7: Migrating from MD5 Password Authentication

PostgreSQL 18 officially deprecates the **md5** password authentication method. While **md5** connections still function in this release, the server now emits deprecation warnings in the log when **md5** authentication is used, controlled by the new **md5_password_warnings** parameter. A future PostgreSQL release will remove **md5** support entirely. In this recipe, we audit our **cookbook_db** cluster for any remaining **md5** usage, migrate all roles to **scram-sha-256**, and verify that the migration is complete.

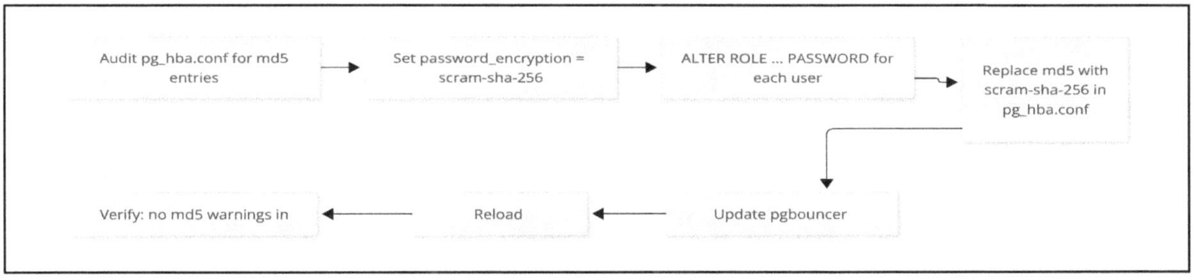

Fig 9.2: MD5 to SCRAM-SHA-256 Migration Workflow

Audit Current Authentication Methods

We begin by identifying all **pg_hba.conf** entries that still reference **md5** and all roles whose stored password hash uses the older MD5 format:

```
sudo grep -n 'md5' /etc/postgresql/18/main/pg_hba.conf
```

We then query the **pg_authid** catalog (as a superuser) to identify roles with MD5-format password hashes. MD5 hashes start with the prefix **md5** followed by 32 hexadecimal characters, while SCRAM hashes start with **SCRAM-SHA-256$**.

So here, following is the quick SQL query:

```
SELECT rolname, left(rolpassword, 10) AS hash_prefix
FROM pg_authid
WHERE rolpassword IS NOT NULL
```

```
  AND rolpassword LIKE 'md5%'
ORDER BY rolname;
```

Any role appearing in this result still uses an MD5 password hash and must be re-encrypted. If no rows are returned, all roles already use SCRAM hashes and we can skip directly to the **pg_hba.conf** update step.

Migrate Roles to SCRAM-SHA-256

We first ensure that the server's **password_encryption** parameter is set to **scram-sha-256**, which controls the hash algorithm used when passwords are set or changed. In PostgreSQL 18, this is already the default, but we can verify it explicitly with the following:

```
SHOW password_encryption;


-- If it shows 'md5', change it:
ALTER SYSTEM SET password_encryption = 'scram-sha-256';
SELECT pg_reload_conf();
```

We now re-set the password for every MD5-authenticated role, which causes PostgreSQL to store the password using the SCRAM-SHA-256 hash. We must know (or reset to) each user's password to perform this step. In the following SQL block, we will for each affected role:

```
ALTER ROLE anika WITH PASSWORD 'anika_secure_pass';
ALTER ROLE rohan WITH PASSWORD 'rohan_secure_pass';
ALTER ROLE priya WITH PASSWORD 'priya_secure_pass';
ALTER ROLE replication_user WITH PASSWORD 'repl_secure_pass';
```

So, let us verify that all roles now use SCRAM hashes by re-running the audit query:

```
SELECT rolname, left(rolpassword, 20) AS hash_prefix
FROM pg_authid
WHERE rolpassword IS NOT NULL
ORDER BY rolname;
```

Every row should now show a **hash_prefix** starting with **SCRAM-SHA-256$**. We then update **pg_hba.conf** to replace all remaining **md5** entries with **scram-sha-256**, as we configured in Recipe #1 of this chapter. We also update the **pgbouncer** configuration from Chapter 3 to set **auth_type = scram-sha-256**, so that the connection pool layer uses the same authentication method.

Verify Migration

After reloading the configuration, we confirm that no **md5** deprecation warnings appear in the server log. We now proceed to enable the warnings parameter and connect with a test user.

At this stage, we will then run the following snippet:

```
# Ensure the warning parameter is active:
sudo -u postgres psql -c "SHOW md5_password_warnings;"

# Connect with a test user and check the log:
psql -h localhost -U anika -d cookbook_db \
    -c "SELECT current_user;"

sudo tail -5 /var/log/postgresql/postgresql-18-main.log
```

The log should contain no **md5**-related warnings, confirming that the entire authentication chain is using **scram-sha-256**. The **md5_password_warnings** parameter defaults to **on** in PostgreSQL 18, so any remaining MD5 usage would produce visible warnings in the log. After we complete this migration, it ensures us a smooth transition when **md5** support is removed in a future release, and it strengthens our security posture immediately because **scram-sha-256** uses salted, iterated hashing that is resistant to rainbow table attacks and credential replay, unlike the weaker MD5 scheme.

Authentication Method	Security Level	Status in PG18
md5	Weak (unsalted, replay-vulnerable)	Deprecated with warnings
scram-sha-256	Strong (salted, iterated, challenge-response)	Default and recommended
ldap	Delegated to directory server	Supported (see Recipe #5)
oauth	Token-based (bearer tokens from IdP)	New in PostgreSQL 18 (see Recipe #6)
cert	Mutual TLS with client certificates	Supported (see Recipe #2)

Summary

This chapter secured our **cookbook_db** application at every authentication, encryption, and audit layer. We managed roles and schema-level permissions using **scram-sha-256** as the default authentication method, and we highlighted the PostgreSQL 18 behavioral change where **AFTER** triggers now execute as the role active at queue time rather than commit time, which strengthens audit trail accuracy. We generated SSL certificates and configured encrypted connections, encrypted database exports at rest using AES-256 with OpenSSL, and deployed **pgAudit** alongside a trigger-based audit mechanism that feeds our **public.event_log** table with time-ordered **uuidv7()** identifiers from Chapter 8.

We integrated LDAP for centralized directory authentication and then configured the native OAuth 2.0 authentication via the SASL **OAUTHBEARER** mechanism. This feature enables our database to accept bearer tokens from external identity providers, eliminating static passwords for token-authenticated connections and integrating with enterprise SSO infrastructure. Finally, we completed the migration from the deprecated **md5** authentication method to **scram-sha-256** across all roles, **pg_hba.conf** entries, and connection pool configurations.

CHAPTER 10
IMPLEMENTING DATABASE BACKUP STRATEGIES

Introduction

This chapter equips us with the backup strategies that protect our **cookbook_db** application against data loss, corruption, and operational failures. We will start by automating daily backups with a shell script and **cron**, building on the scripting patterns we established in Chapter 8 Recipe #2. We will then configure continuous archiving to enable Point-in-Time Recovery (PITR) using the WAL archive infrastructure we built in Chapter 5.

From there, we will work with **pg_probackup** for fine-grained instance management and **pgBackRest** for repository-based backup orchestration with built-in compression, encryption, and parallelism. We will implement both incremental and differential backup strategies that capture only the changes since the last full backup, optimizing storage consumption and backup duration. Finally, we will perform schema-level backups that selectively target our **hr**, **sales**, and **production** schemas for situations where a full-cluster backup is unnecessary.

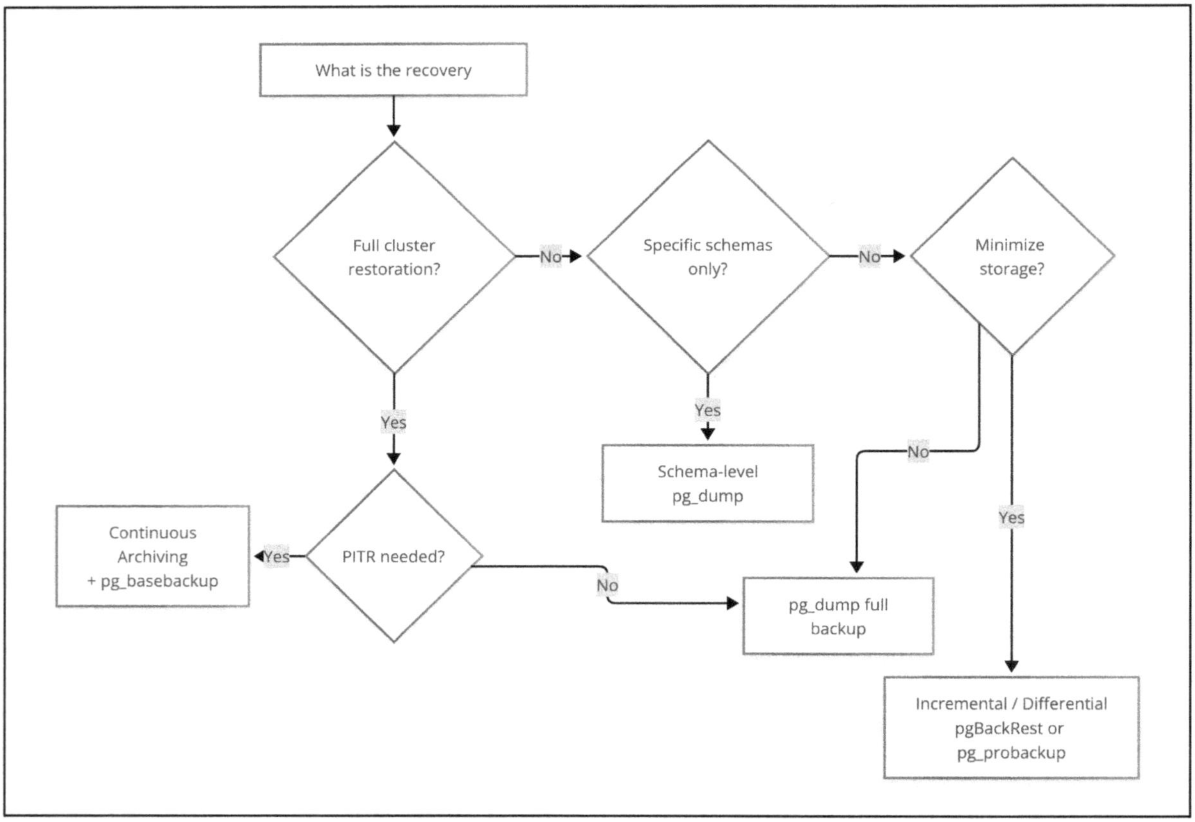

Fig 10.1: Backup Strategy Decision Map

Recipe #1: Automating Database Backup

Automated backups are the first line of defense against data loss. In this recipe, we create a production-grade backup script that dumps our **cookbook_db** database in custom format, timestamps the output file, rotates old backups based on a retention policy, and optionally uploads the archive to the S3 bucket we configured in Chapter 3. We schedule the script with **cron** for unattended daily execution.

Create Backup Script

Here, we will create a script named **cookbook_backup.sh** in the home directory of the **postgres** system user. We can now write the following content:

```
#!/bin/bash
set -euo pipefail

# — Configuration ——————————————————————————
DB_NAME="cookbook_db"
BACKUP_DIR="/var/backups/postgresql"
RETENTION_DAYS=14
TIMESTAMP=$(date +%Y%m%d_%H%M%S)
DUMP_FILE="${BACKUP_DIR}/${DB_NAME}_${TIMESTAMP}.dump"
LOG_FILE="${BACKUP_DIR}/backup.log"

# — Create directory if missing ————————————
mkdir -p "${BACKUP_DIR}"

# — Perform the backup ——————————————————
echo "[$(date)] Starting backup of ${DB_NAME}" >> "${LOG_FILE}"

pg_dump -Fc -Z 6 -d "${DB_NAME}" -f "${DUMP_FILE}"

if [ $? -eq 0 ]; then
    DUMP_SIZE=$(du -h "${DUMP_FILE}" | cut -f1)
    echo "[$(date)] Backup completed: ${DUMP_FILE} (${DUMP_SIZE})"
\
         >> "${LOG_FILE}"
```

```
else
    echo "[$(date)] ERROR: Backup failed for ${DB_NAME}" \
         >> "${LOG_FILE}"
    exit 1
fi

# — Rotate old backups ——————————————————
find "${BACKUP_DIR}" -name "${DB_NAME}_*.dump" \
    -type f -mtime +${RETENTION_DAYS} -delete

echo "[$(date)] Rotation complete. Retained ${RETENTION_DAYS}
days." \
     >> "${LOG_FILE}"
```

The **-Fc** flag produces a custom-format archive that supports selective restoration by schema and table, which we will use in Recipe #5. The **-Z 6** flag applies zlib compression at level 6 (a good balance between speed and size). The **RETENTION_DAYS** variable controls how many days of backup files are retained before the rotation step deletes them.

So here, we will then run the following code:

```
chmod +x /var/lib/postgresql/cookbook_backup.sh
sudo -u postgres /var/lib/postgresql/cookbook_backup.sh

# Verify the backup file exists:
ls -lh /var/backups/postgresql/
```

The output lists the new dump file with its timestamp and compressed size, confirming the backup completed successfully.

We will also verify the dump integrity by listing its table of contents:

```
pg_restore --list /var/backups/postgresql/cookbook_db_*.dump | head
-20
```

Schedule with cron

We schedule the script to run daily at 01:00 AM using the **postgres** user's crontab:

```
sudo -u postgres crontab -e

# Add the following entry:
0 1 * * * /var/lib/postgresql/cookbook_backup.sh
```

The cron daemon runs the script every night at 01:00 AM, creating a timestamped dump and deleting any archives older than 14 days. We can verify that the cron entry is registered by running **crontab -l** as the **postgres** user. If we also want to upload the dump to the S3 bucket from Chapter 3, we add an **aws s3 cp** command at the end of the script, referencing the **cookbook-db-backups** bucket we created there.

We do not repeat the S3 configuration here, as it was covered in Chapter 3 Recipe #2.

Test Backup and Restore

We will now validate the backup by restoring it into a temporary database and verifying that every schema and table arrived intact.

```
# Create a temporary test database:
sudo -u postgres createdb cookbook_db_test

# Restore the backup:
sudo -u postgres pg_restore \
    -d cookbook_db_test \
    /var/backups/postgresql/cookbook_db_*.dump

# Verify schemas and row counts:
sudo -u postgres psql -d cookbook_db_test -c "\dn"
sudo -u postgres psql -d cookbook_db_test \
    -c "SELECT count(*) FROM hr.employees;"
sudo -u postgres psql -d cookbook_db_test \
    -c "SELECT count(*) FROM sales.orders;"

# Drop the test database:
sudo -u postgres dropdb cookbook_db_test
```

The schema listing must show **public**, **hr**, **sales**, and **production**, and the row counts must match the source database at the time of backup. We should incorporate this restore-and-verify step into a weekly automated test to confirm that our backups are genuinely recoverable, not just successfully created.

Recipe #2: Executing Continuous Archiving PostgreSQL Backup

Continuous archiving combines a base backup with an ongoing stream of archived WAL segments to enable Point-in-Time Recovery (PITR). This approach allows us to restore our **cookbook_db** database to any specific moment within the archive retention window, not just to the time of the last **pg_dump**. As we configured **archive_mode**, **archive_command**, and **wal_level** in Chapter 5, we refer back to those settings here and focus on creating the base backup and performing a point-in-time restore.

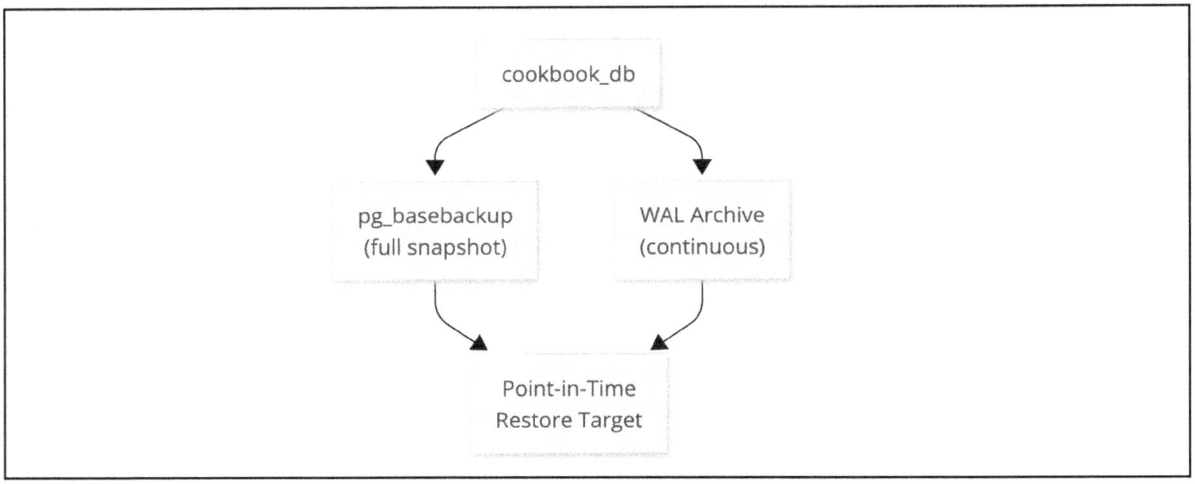

Fig 10.2: Continuous Archiving and PITR Data Flow

Create Base Backup

In the following script, we will use **pg_basebackup** to create a full snapshot of the running cluster. This base backup, combined with the WAL archive, provides the foundation for PITR as shown below:

```
sudo -u postgres pg_basebackup \
    -D /var/backups/postgresql/base_backup \
    -Ft -Xs -P \
    -U postgres
```

The **-Ft** flag produces a tar-format archive, **-Xs** streams the WAL files needed for consistency into the backup, and **-P** displays progress. After the command completes, the **/var/backups/postgresql/base_backup** directory contains **base.tar** and **pg_wal.tar**, which together represent the entire cluster at the time of backup. With this in mind, we will now verify the backup contents:

```
ls -lh /var/backups/postgresql/base_backup/
```

The terminal will show:

```
total 52M
-rw------- 1 postgres postgres  49M Apr 25 01:15 base.tar
-rw------- 1 postgres postgres 3.2M Apr 25 01:15 pg_wal.tar
```

Perform Point-in-Time Recovery

We simulate a data loss scenario and recover to a specific timestamp using the base backup and archived WAL files. We first record a reference timestamp, insert a row, then delete it to simulate the loss, and finally recover to the moment just before the deletion. At this stage, we will then run the following SQL to note the safe recovery target:

```
-- Note the current timestamp as our recovery target:
SELECT now() AS recovery_target;

-- Insert a row we want to preserve:
INSERT INTO hr.employees (first_name, last_name, email,
    department, salary)
VALUES ('Recovery', 'TestUser', 'recovery@techparts.io',
    'Engineering', 85000.00);

-- Simulate accidental deletion (this is the event we recover
from):
DELETE FROM hr.employees
WHERE email = 'recovery@techparts.io';
```

We will now stop the server, restore the base backup, configure recovery to our target timestamp, and start the server:

```
sudo systemctl stop postgresql

# Preserve the current data directory for safety:
sudo mv /var/lib/postgresql/18/main \
        /var/lib/postgresql/18/main_backup

# Restore from the base backup:
sudo mkdir -p /var/lib/postgresql/18/main
sudo tar xf /var/backups/postgresql/base_backup/base.tar \
    -C /var/lib/postgresql/18/main
sudo tar xf /var/backups/postgresql/base_backup/pg_wal.tar \
    -C /var/lib/postgresql/18/main/pg_wal/

# Set ownership:
sudo chown -R postgres:postgres /var/lib/postgresql/18/main

# Configure recovery target:
sudo -u postgres bash -c "cat >>
/var/lib/postgresql/18/main/postgresql.conf << 'EOF'
restore_command = 'cp /var/lib/postgresql/wal_archive/%f %p'
recovery_target_time = '<RECOVERY_TIMESTAMP>'
recovery_target_action = 'promote'
EOF"

# Create the recovery signal file:
sudo -u postgres touch /var/lib/postgresql/18/main/recovery.signal

# Start the server in recovery mode:
sudo systemctl start postgresql
```

After the server starts, it replays WAL records from the archive up to the **recovery_target_time** we specified, then promotes itself to a normal primary. We can now verify that the recovery succeeded by checking for our test row. So here, we will then run the following SQL:

```
SELECT * FROM hr.employees
WHERE email = 'recovery@techparts.io';
```

If the recovery target was set correctly (to a moment after the insert but before the delete), the row exists, confirming that PITR recovered the data successfully. Here, we will remove the recovery parameters from **postgresql.conf** after verification to prevent the server from re-entering recovery mode on the next restart.

Recipe #3: Working with pg_probackup and pgBackRest

Enterprise environments require backup tools that go beyond **pg_dump** and **pg_basebackup** by offering incremental backups, backup validation, parallel processing, and retention management. In this recipe, we configure both **pg_probackup** and **pgBackRest** against our **cookbook_db** cluster and demonstrate full and incremental backup workflows for each tool.

Using 'pg_probackup'

We will then install **pg_probackup** and initialize a backup catalog:

```
sudo apt install -y pg-probackup-18


# Initialize the backup catalog:
sudo -u postgres pg_probackup init \
    -B /var/backups/pg_probackup


# Add our cookbook_db instance:
sudo -u postgres pg_probackup add-instance \
    -B /var/backups/pg_probackup \
    --instance=cookbook \
    --pgdata=/var/lib/postgresql/18/main
```

We will now create a full backup with compression enabled:

```
sudo -u postgres pg_probackup backup \
```

```
    -B /var/backups/pg_probackup \
    --instance=cookbook \
    --backup-mode=full \
    --compress \
    --stream \
    --threads=4
```

The **--stream** flag includes WAL in the backup without depending on the archive, and **--threads=4** parallelizes the file copy across four workers. At this stage, we will validate the backup integrity:

```
sudo -u postgres pg_probackup validate \
    -B /var/backups/pg_probackup \
    --instance=cookbook
```

Using 'pgBackRest'

So, let us install **pgBackRest** and create a stanza configuration for our cluster:

```
sudo apt install -y pgbackrest
```

Next, we proceed to create configuration file at **/etc/pgbackrest/pgbackrest.conf**:

```
[global]
repo1-path=/var/backups/pgbackrest
repo1-retention-full=2
repo1-cipher-type=aes-256-cbc
repo1-cipher-pass=<ENCRYPTION_PASSPHRASE>
process-max=4
compress-type=zst

[cookbook]
pg1-path=/var/lib/postgresql/18/main
```

The **repo1-cipher-type** and **repo1-cipher-pass** settings encrypt every backup file at rest using AES-256, complementing the transport-level encryption we configured in Chapter 9. The **compress-type=zst** setting uses Zstandard compression for the best compression ratio at high speed.

Here, we will initialize the stanza and create a full backup:

```
sudo -u postgres pgbackrest --stanza=cookbook stanza-create
sudo -u postgres pgbackrest --stanza=cookbook \
    --type=full backup
```

Next, we will then verify the backup:

```
sudo -u postgres pgbackrest --stanza=cookbook check
```

The check confirms that the WAL archive is accessible, the stanza configuration is valid, and the latest backup is consistent. Both tools are now ready for the incremental and differential workflows we will configure in Recipe #4.

Feature	**pg_probackup**	**pgBackRest**
Installation	pg-probackup-18 package	pgbackrest package
Incremental mode	--backup-mode=delta (page-level)	--type=incr (file-level)
Differential mode	--backup-mode=diff	--type=diff
Compression	--compress (zlib)	compress-type=zst (Zstandard)
Encryption at rest	Not built-in	repo1-cipher-type=aes-256-cbc
Parallelism	--threads=N	process-max=N
PITR restore	--recovery-target-time	--target (timestamp or LSN)

Recipe #4: Performing Incremental and Differential Backups

Full backups capture the entire cluster, but on large databases they consume significant storage and time. Incremental backups capture only the data that changed since the last backup of any type, while differential backups capture all changes since the last full backup. Both strategies reduce storage consumption and backup duration while maintaining the ability to restore to any point covered by the backup chain. In this recipe, we implement both strategies using the tools we configured in Recipe #3.

Incremental Backups with 'pgBackRest'

An incremental backup with **`pgBackRest`** captures only the files that changed since the last backup (whether full, differential, or incremental).

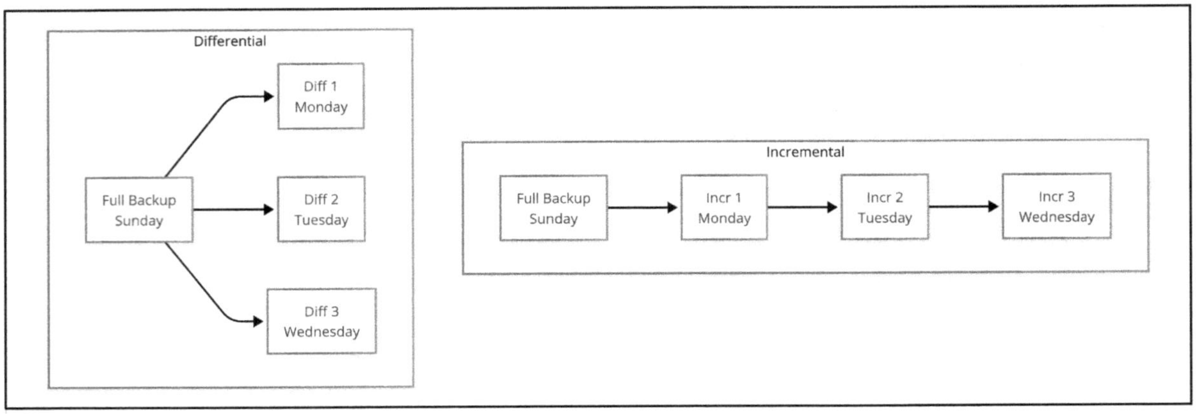

Fig 10.3: Incremental vs Differential Backup Chain

Let us now create an incremental backup after the full backup from Recipe #3:

```
sudo -u postgres pgbackrest --stanza=cookbook \
    --type=incr backup
```

At this point, we will generate some write activity in **`cookbook_db`** to ensure there are changes to capture, then take another incremental:

```
# Generate changes:
sudo -u postgres psql -d cookbook_db -c \
    "UPDATE sales.orders SET total_due = total_due * 1.01
     WHERE territory = 'South Asia';"


# Take another incremental:
sudo -u postgres pgbackrest --stanza=cookbook \
    --type=incr backup


# List all backups in the repository:
sudo -u postgres pgbackrest --stanza=cookbook info
```

The info output shows the full backup and the two incrementals, each with their size and timestamp. To restore to a specific point using the incremental chain, **`pgBackRest`** automatically identifies and applies the correct sequence of backups (full plus each incremental in order).

So, let us run the following restore command:

```
sudo systemctl stop postgresql

sudo -u postgres pgbackrest --stanza=cookbook \
    --delta \
    --target="<TARGET_TIMESTAMP>" \
    --target-action=promote \
    restore

sudo systemctl start postgresql
```

The **--delta** option applies only the changed files, making the restore process faster than a full restore. The **--target** parameter specifies the PITR timestamp, and **--target-action=promote** brings the server online as a primary after recovery completes.

Differential Backups with 'pg_probackup'

A differential backup with **pg_probackup** captures all page-level changes since the last full backup, regardless of any intervening incremental or differential backups. This means a differential restore requires only the full backup plus the single differential, simplifying the restore chain.

With this in mind, we will now create a differential backup:

```
sudo -u postgres pg_probackup backup \
    -B /var/backups/pg_probackup \
    --instance=cookbook \
    --backup-mode=diff \
    --compress \
    --stream \
    --threads=4
```

At this stage, we will then validate the differential backup and list all available backups:

```
sudo -u postgres pg_probackup validate \
    -B /var/backups/pg_probackup \
    --instance=cookbook
```

```
sudo -u postgres pg_probackup show \
    -B /var/backups/pg_probackup \
    --instance=cookbook
```

The show output lists the full backup and the differential with their backup IDs, sizes, and timestamps. To restore a specific differential backup, we reference its backup ID directly as below:

```
sudo systemctl stop postgresql


sudo -u postgres pg_probackup restore \
    -B /var/backups/pg_probackup \
    --instance=cookbook \
    -D /var/lib/postgresql/18/main \
    -i <BACKUP_ID>


sudo systemctl start postgresql
```

The **pg_probackup** utility automatically locates the parent full backup and applies the differential on top of it, restoring the cluster to the exact state captured by the differential. After the restore, we verify our **cookbook_db** schemas and row counts as we have done in previous recipes.

Recipe #5: Executing Schema-Level Backup

Schema-level backups allow us to selectively target specific schemas within **cookbook_db** rather than backing up the entire cluster. This approach is valuable when only certain schemas contain actively changing data, when we need to migrate a subset of the database to a different environment, or when storage constraints require selective backups. In this recipe, we back up the **hr**, **sales**, and **production** schemas independently and restore them to a test database.

Create Schema-Level Backups

So here, we will then use **pg_dump** with the **-n** flag to select specific schemas. We will then create separate backup files for each schema group to maintain maximum restoration flexibility:

```
# Create the backup directory:
sudo mkdir -p /var/backups/postgresql/schema_backups
```

```
# Back up the hr schema:
sudo -u postgres pg_dump -Fc -Z 6 \
    -n hr -d cookbook_db \
    -f /var/backups/postgresql/schema_backups/hr_schema.dump

# Back up the sales schema (includes partitions):
sudo -u postgres pg_dump -Fc -Z 6 \
    -n sales -d cookbook_db \
    -f /var/backups/postgresql/schema_backups/sales_schema.dump

# Back up the production schema:
sudo -u postgres pg_dump -Fc -Z 6 \
    -n production -d cookbook_db \
    -f
/var/backups/postgresql/schema_backups/production_schema.dump

# Verify the backup files:
ls -lh /var/backups/postgresql/schema_backups/
```

Each dump file contains only the objects (tables, indexes, sequences, functions, triggers) belonging to the specified schema. The **`sales`** schema backup includes all partition children (**`orders_2025`**, **`orders_2026`**, etc.) because declarative partitions reside in the same schema as their parent. If we need to back up multiple schemas in a single file, we can chain **`-n`** flags:

```
# Combined backup of hr and sales in a single file:
sudo -u postgres pg_dump -Fc -Z 6 \
    -n hr -n sales -d cookbook_db \
    -f
/var/backups/postgresql/schema_backups/hr_sales_combined.dump
```

Restore and Verify Schema Backups

We restore the schema-level backups into a test database and verify the object inventory and row counts with the following:

```
# Create a test database:
```

```
sudo -u postgres createdb cookbook_schema_test

# Restore the hr schema:
sudo -u postgres pg_restore \
    -d cookbook_schema_test \
    /var/backups/postgresql/schema_backups/hr_schema.dump

# Restore the sales schema:
sudo -u postgres pg_restore \
    -d cookbook_schema_test \
    /var/backups/postgresql/schema_backups/sales_schema.dump

# Verify:
sudo -u postgres psql -d cookbook_schema_test << 'EOF'
\dn
\dt hr.*
\dt sales.*
SELECT count(*) AS hr_employees FROM hr.employees;
SELECT count(*) AS sales_orders FROM sales.orders;
EOF

# Clean up:
sudo -u postgres dropdb cookbook_schema_test
```

The schema listing must show **hr** and **sales**, and the row counts must match the source database at the time of backup. If we need to restore only a single table from within a schema backup, we can use the **pg_restore -t** flag to target it selectively. For example, **pg_restore -d target_db -t employees hr_schema.dump** restores only the **employees** table from the **hr** schema backup. This granularity is one of the key advantages of the custom-format (**-Fc**) archive that we use consistently throughout our backup strategy.

Summary

This chapter equipped our **cookbook_db** application with a comprehensive backup infrastructure spanning five complementary strategies. We automated daily backups with a production-grade shell script that produces timestamped custom-format archives, applies retention-based rotation, and integrates with the S3 upload workflow from Chapter 3. We configured continuous archiving for Point-in-Time Recovery, combining the WAL archive from Chapter 5 with a **pg_basebackup** snapshot and demonstrating a full PITR workflow that recovered an accidentally deleted row to a specific timestamp.

We deployed both **pg_probackup** and **pgBackRest** as enterprise-grade backup tools, configuring full, incremental, and differential backup strategies for each. The **pgBackRest** configuration includes AES-256 encryption at rest and Zstandard compression, while **pg_probackup** provides page-level delta tracking for minimal storage consumption. We also performed schema-level backups that selectively target individual schemas within **cookbook_db**, demonstrating the flexibility of the custom-format archive for granular restoration.

CHAPTER 11
PERFORM DATABASE RECOVERY & RESTORATION

Introduction

In this chapter, you will be learning advanced database recovery and restoration techniques for PostgreSQL. You will be exploring how to perform full and point-in-time recovery to restore databases to a previous state in the event of data loss or corruption. This includes configuring continuous archiving, creating base backups, and using WAL files to recover the database to a specific point in time. By mastering these techniques, you will enhance your ability to recover from unexpected data issues effectively.

You will also be delving into the use of Barman for advanced recovery scenarios, including tablespace and table recovery. This will involve restoring individual tablespaces or specific tables without affecting the rest of the database, providing flexibility and precision in data recovery. You will learn to mark backups for restoration, use Barman commands for targeted recovery, and ensure data integrity through careful verification processes.

Additionally, you will focus on schema-level restoration, which allows you to recover specific schemas from backups, minimizing downtime and preserving the integrity of your database environment. Finally, you will be learning to monitor restore operations using Barman. It helps to track progress and troubleshoot any issues that arise during the recovery process.

Recipe #1: Performing Full and Point-in-Time Recovery

The execution of a full recovery or Point-in-Time Recovery (PITR) restores databases to a previous state in the event of data loss or corruption. This recipe will demonstrate both recovery processes using the database.

Full Recovery

Before starting a full recovery, we will check if we have a complete backup of the database. We will use the **pg_dump** to create a backup if you don't have one:

```
pg_dump -U your_user -W -F t adventureworks >
adventureworks_backup.tar
```

The backup will be saved as a tar file.

Next, we remove the existing database to prepare for recovery:

```
dropdb -U your_user adventureworks
```

After this, we then recreate the database with the same name as the original:

```
createdb -U your_user adventureworks
```

And then, we use **pg_restore** to restore the backup to the newly created database:

```
pg_restore -U your_user -d adventureworks -F t
adventureworks_backup.tar
```

After the restore process is complete, your database will be fully recovered to the state captured in the backup file.

Point-in-Time Recovery

Now here, at first, we will enable the continuous archiving in the **postgresql.conf** file:

```
wal_level = replica

archive_mode = on

archive_command = 'cp %p /path/to/archive/%f'
```

While doing this, we must ensure thaa the **wal_level** is set to **replica**, and so we must adjust **archive_command** to copy WAL files to your chosen archive directory. And then, we apply the configuration changes by restarting the server:

```
sudo systemctl restart postgresql
```

Next, we then use **pg_basebackup** to create a snapshot of the database:

```
pg_basebackup -U your_user -D /path/to/backup -Ft -Xs -P
```

Now, to restore to a specific point in time, we will start PostgreSQL in recovery mode:

```
standby_mode = on

primary_conninfo = 'host=localhost port=5432 user=your_user'

restore_command = 'cp /path/to/archive/%f "%p"'

recovery_target_time = 'YYYY-MM-DD HH:MI:SS'
```

After this, we then create a **recovery.conf** file with these contents in the data directory and specify the target time for recovery. And then, we execute the following to start PostgreSQL in recovery mode:

```
pg_ctl start -D /path/to/data -w -t 600
```

The server will apply WAL files until it reaches the specified target time, allowing the database to be consistent at that point. Once the database reaches the target time, you can use it as usual. But, don't forget to keep WAL files secure, as they are key to the PITR process.

Recipe #2: Restoring Database using Barman

Barman is a robust tool for managing PostgreSQL backups and restorations. It supports incremental and differential restores. This recipe combines restoring databases with Barman, focusing on utilizing incremental and differential backups for efficiency.

Perform Backup

To begin with, we will first list the available backups for the database using Barman:

```
barman list-backup adventureworks
```

Here, we will identify the backup you wish to restore, noting the backup ID. And then, mark the selected full backup as restored to prepare for recovery:

```
barman mark-restore adventureworks full_backup_id
```

After this, we create a directory to store the restored database temporarily:

```
mkdir /path/to/restore
```

And then, we restore the full backup using Barman:

```
barman recover --remote-ssh-command "ssh user@your_server" --
target-directory /path/to/restore adventureworks full_backup_id
```

While doing so, just replace **`user@your_server`** and **`full_backup_id`** with appropriate values. If an incremental or differential backup is available, we can mark it as restored and apply it:

```
barman mark-restore adventureworks incremental_backup_id
barman recover --remote-ssh-command "ssh user@your_server" --
target-directory /path/to/restore --delta adventureworks
incremental_backup_id
```

This whole process applies changes since the full backup, minimizing data restoration time.

Start PostgreSQL in Recovery Mode

To begin with, we will first start the PostgreSQL server in recovery mode to apply archived WAL files:

```
pg_ctl -D /path/to/restore start
```

We will keep monitoring the recovery progress via log files:

```
tail -f /path/to/restore/pg_log/postgresql-<date>.log
```

Once the recovery is complete, we then stop the PostgreSQL server:

```
pg_ctl -D /path/to/restore stop
```

After this, we then synchronize the restored database with the original data directory:

```
rsync -av /path/to/restore/ /var/lib/postgresql/data/
```

Here, we need to ensure ownership permissions are correct:

```
chown -R postgres:postgres /var/lib/postgresql/data/
```

Restart PostgreSQL

Next, we then restart the PostgreSQL server:

```
systemctl start postgresql
```

And finally, we connect to the restored database and verify data integrity:

```
psql -U postgres adventureworks
```

With this, by utilizing Barman for incremental and differential restores, we were able to enhance the recovery process for the database, and able to achieve efficient data restoration with minimal downtime and storage usage.

Recipe #3: Performing Tablespace and Table Recovery

Tablespaces allow us to manage the physical storage of database objects, while individual table recovery restores specific tables without affecting the rest of the database. This recipe will demonstrate performing tablespace and table recovery using Barman for the database.

Tablespace Recovery

To start with, we will first list the available backups for the database using Barman:

```
barman list-backup adventureworks
```

Here, we will identify the backup containing the tablespace you need to recover and note its ID. And then we will mark the selected backup as ready for restoration:

```
barman mark-restore adventureworks backup_id
```

After this, we then create a directory to temporarily store the restored tablespace:

```
mkdir /path/to/restore
```

We will use Barman then to restore the tablespace:

```
barman recover-tablespace --remote-ssh-command "ssh
user@your_server" --target-directory /path/to/restore --tablespace-
name your_tablespace_name adventureworks backup_id
```

And then, we will copy the restored tablespace to its original location on the server:

```
rsync -av /path/to/restore/ /var/lib/postgresql/data/pg_tblspc/
```

After this, we then restart the PostgreSQL service to apply changes:

```
systemctl restart postgresql
```

Table Recovery

The first thing we will do, is to check available backups for the database:

```
barman list-backup adventureworks
```

We will mark the desired backup for restoration:

```
barman mark-restore adventureworks backup_id
```

After this, we then create a directory to hold the restored table:

```
mkdir /path/to/restore
```

And we then restore the table using Barman:

```
barman recover-table --remote-ssh-command "ssh user@your_server" --
target-directory /path/to/restore --tablespace-name
your_tablespace_name adventureworks backup_id your_table_name
```

In the database, we then recreate the table structure using **psql**:

```
psql -U postgres -d adventureworks -c "CREATE TABLE your_table_name
(LIKE your_table_name INCLUDING ALL);"
```

Next, we use **pg_restore** to load data into the new table:

```
pg_restore --data-only --table=your_table_name --
dbname=adventureworks /path/to/restore/your_table_name.sql
```

Finally, we confirm the data restoration by querying the table:

```
psql -U postgres -d adventureworks -c "SELECT COUNT(*) FROM
your_table_name;"
```

These instructions let you use Barman to successfully perform tablespace and table recovery for the database, guaranteeing accurate data management and restoration.

Recipe #4: Performing Schema-Level Restore

A schema-level restore allows you to recover individual schemas from a backup without affecting the rest of the database, providing flexibility in managing database objects. This recipe will demonstrate performing a schema-level restore for the database using Barman.

Select and Mark Backup for Restoration

Here to, we will first list all backups available for the database:

```
barman list-backup adventureworks
```

We then identify the backup containing the schema you need to restore. Mark the backup as restored to prepare it for schema-level recovery:

```
barman mark-restore adventureworks backup_id
```

After this, we then set up a temporary directory to hold the restored schema:

```
mkdir /path/to/restore
```

Schema Restoration

We will again use Barman to recover the schema:

```
barman recover-schema --remote-ssh-command "ssh user@your_server" -
-target-directory /path/to/restore --tablespace-name
your_tablespace_name adventureworks backup_id your_schema_name
```

Next, we create a new schema in the database using **pg_restore**:

```
pg_restore --schema-only --dbname=adventureworks
/path/to/restore/your_schema_name.sql
```

And then, we need to confirm the schema restoration by listing its contents:

```
psql -U postgres -d adventureworks -c "\d your_schema_name.*;"
```

This query verifies that all objects within the schema are restored correctly. You gained flexibility and reduced restoration downtime by performing a schema-level restore on specific database parts.

Recipe #5: Monitoring Restore Operations

The monitoring of the restore operations can assure the success and efficiency of database recovery processes. The Barman provides several tools to track the status and progress of restore operations. This recipe will demonstrate monitoring restore operations for the database using Barman.

View Restore Logs

This lists all restore operations for the database:

```
barman list-restore adventureworks
```

This command shows ongoing and completed restores, including their status and target directories. Then, use Barman to display the progress of a specific restore operation:

```
barman show-restore adventureworks restore_id
```

This displays the status and progress, including files restored and estimated time remaining. Followed by, check the log messages for detailed information on the restore process:

```
barman show-restore-logs adventureworks restore_id
```

It outputs log entries, providing insights into errors, warnings, or other critical events during restoration.

Verify Successful Restoration

If needed, we can halt a restore operation in progress:

```
barman stop-restore adventureworks restore_id
```

Now here, stopping a restore operation removes the restore lock and cancels the ongoing process. After completion, we can also verify the restored database by connecting and executing test queries:

```
psql -U postgres -d adventureworks
```

We can also onduct queries to ensure data integrity and proper functionality.

Summary

All things considered, you gained knowledge of sophisticated PostgreSQL database recovery and restoration methods in this chapter. You learned setting up continuous archiving, making base backups, and utilizing WAL files to restore the database to a particular point in time in order to accomplish full and point-in-time recovery (PITR). Furthermore, you learned how to use Barman for tablespace and table recovery, enabling you to restore database objects without compromising the database. This required data integrity verification, backup marking, and targeted recovery with Barman commands.

Schema-level restoration was also covered in the chapter, allowing you to precisely manage complex recovery scenarios and recover individual schemas. You gained knowledge on how to replicate schema structures, validate the restoration procedure, and restore schemas using Barman. Lastly, you explored monitoring restore operations with Barman, learning how to keep tabs on developments and troubleshoot problems while the system is recovering. Overall, this chapter gave you the knowledge and abilities needed to successfully recover and restore data in PostgreSQL.

Index

A

B

C

D

E

R

S

Epilogue

If you've made it this far and tried out a few of the recipes, congratulations - you're not the same database pro who started on page one. The cookbook_db application that you built alongside the chapters is more than just a teaching tool. It's a working model of a real production system, complete with replicated nodes, audit trails, encrypted backups and recovery procedures that you've personally executed. Now you've got that experience. You can't unlearn it, and it'll resurface every time you face a similar challenge in the wild.

I want to leave you with three things I've learned from writing this book. Firstly, PostgreSQL ***rewards patience***. When you're under pressure, it's tempting to rush things. Just restart the service. Just drop the slot. Just rebuild the index. But in almost all cases, the better move is to read the log first, check the relevant system view, and let the database tell you what it needs. PostgreSQL is straightforward about this. It'll tell you about replication lag in pg_stat_replication, vacuum delay in pg_stat_progress_vacuum, and authentication failures in the server log, every time, without fail. The admins I admire most are the ones who slow down precisely when others speed up, because they trust the database to guide them.

The second thing to remember is that ***automation pays for itself in ways*** you can't see. Whatever shell script we wrote, every cron schedule, every PL/pgSQL function that creates next month's partition before we even need it, all of these things contribute to a system that runs quietly when we're not using it. Quiet systems are happy systems. They give us the chance to think about how to improve things for next time instead of always trying to fix the problems that have already happened. So, if you're thinking about investing in automation early on in a database's life, that's one of the best decisions you can make as a team. And trust me, it'll get harder, not easier, if you leave it until later.

The third thing to remember is that the ***PostgreSQL community is the real driving force behind everything*** in this book. Every feature we talked about, from asynchronous I/O to temporal constraints to OAuth authentication, was contributed by people who chose to spend their evenings and weekends improving a piece of software that anyone in the world can use without paying a license fee. When we use PostgreSQL well, we honour that gift. When we contribute back, whether through bug reports, documentation patches, conference talks, or simply mentoring a colleague who is new to the system, we keep the cycle going.

What happens next is your call. Maybe you'll take these recipes back to your production cluster and apply them this week. You might even find yourself using this book as a reference for years, reaching for it whenever you need it. You might find a recipe that doesn't quite fit your situation and come up with something better on your own. All of these are good outcomes.

The best databases are run by people who are always learning, and the best books are the ones that make their readers better than the author ever was.

Thank You

www.ingramcontent.com/pod-product-compliance
Lightning Source LLC
Chambersburg PA
CBHW080212170726
48282CB00030B/1087
* 9 7 8 9 3 4 9 1 7 4 6 3 4 *